best loved

prayers
& words
of wisdom

best loved

prayers
& words
of wisdom

Compiled by Martin H. Manser

Associate Editor: Nicola L. Bull

Collins

Collins

A division of HarperCollins*Publishers*

77–85 Fulham Palace Road, London W6 8JB

www.collins.co.uk

First published in Great Britain in 2009 by HarperCollinsPublishers

2

A catalogue record for this book is available from the British Library.

ISBN 978 000 727894 7

Typeset by M.A.T.S., Southend-on-Sea, Essex

Printed and bound in Great Britain by Clays Ltd, St Ives plc

best loved

prayers
& words
of wisdom

Compiled by Martin H. Manser

Associate Editor: Nicola L. Bull

Collins

Collins

A division of HarperCollins*Publishers*

77–85 Fulham Palace Road, London W6 8JB

www.collins.co.uk

First published in Great Britain in 2009 by HarperCollinsPublishers

2

Copyright © Martin Manser 2009

Martin Manser asserts the moral right to be identified as the editor of this work.

A catalogue record for this book is available from the British Library.

ISBN 978 000 727894 7

Typeset by M.A.T.S., Southend-on-Sea, Essex
Printed and bound in Great Britain by Clays Ltd, St Ives plc

CONDITIONS OF SALE

Contents

Introduction

We live in an age that demands quick fixes to problems and immediate answers to difficulties. Alongside such a desire for instant solutions to major issues, another, deeper, desire surfaces from time to time. Such a longing recognizes that at least some of our difficulties can be resolved by looking at lasting, time-honoured values of human experience and wisdom such as faith in God through Jesus Christ, the importance of prayer, love and service, strength of character, integrity, loyalty and humility.

As we explore for ourselves what generations before us have discovered as the qualities of being human, we realize afresh we are not alone but many before us have trodden a similar path. Our task then is to stop and listen, to follow in their footsteps, to move in the direction they point us to, to apply the principles that underpinned their lives to our own way of living.

We have had in mind two kinds of readers as we have compiled this collection of readings, prayers and quotations. First, those planning a gathering such as a wedding or a funeral who are looking beyond mere quick 'sound bites' to more profound wisdom. Secondly, those who are seeking for deeper meaning and purpose in life or who want inspiration above the ordinary daily routine.

Each reading is given an introduction which sets its background or gives interesting or helpful information. All the readings are arranged in alphabetical order of title (ignoring 'A' or 'The' at the beginning of a title). For ease of reference there are also indexes to help you locate a particular reading.

The voices of the speakers and writers quoted in these pages echo to us through the ages to say, 'There is more to life than your present experience.' Our desire is that we will all not only stop and listen but also respond to the message given here so that we will find the refreshment, peace and light for our own journey that we can then pass on to others.

Martin H. Manser
Nicola L. Bull

Author Index

Author Index

	An evening prayer
	What do I love?
Baillie, John	Evening prayer
Barclay, William	Prayer for humility
Basil of Caesarea	Marks of a Christian
Bass, Dorothy C	Time as gift
Baxter, Richard	Daily seeking after God
	Meek and lowly
Beecher, Henry Ward	Steer by the Bible
Benedict of Nursia	The help of God
Bernard of Clairvaux	Like a reservoir
	O little Bethlehem
Betjeman, John	Take warning
Blake, William	The Lamb
Bonaventure	Journey into God
Bonhoeffer, Dietrich	Help me to pray
	Thanking God
Bright, William	Deliver us from cold hearts
Brontë, Anne	Last lines
Brooks, Phillips	Looking through the Bible
Browne, R E Charles	What is prayer?
Browning, Elizabeth Barrett	How do I love thee?
Bryan, William Jennings	Immortality
	The miracle of the radish
Bunyan, John	Pilgrim's Progress
	Who would true valour see
Calvin, John	Obedience
Carey, William	Expect great things
Chadwick, Samuel	Prevailing prayer
Chambers, Oswald	Discipleship
	Not to criticise
Chesterton, G K	The donkey
Chrysostom, John	Richer than all men
Clare, John	Nature acknowledges God
Clement of Alexandria	Beauty
	God's first Bible
Coleridge, Mary	Lord of the winds
Colonna, Vittoria	The Cross

Author Index

Author Index

Author Index

Index of Bible References

Index of Bible References

Index of Titles and First Lines

(where the first line differs from the title, the first line appears in italics)

Index of Titles and First Lines

Index of Titles and First Lines

Index of Titles and First Lines

Index of Titles and First Lines

Index of Titles and First Lines

Index of Titles and First Lines

Index of Titles and First Lines

Index of Titles and First Lines

Index of Titles and First Lines

Abandonment to God

Charles de Foucauld was born into an aristocratic family in France and lost his faith at a young age. In his twenties he had a powerful religious experience and from then on he dedicated his life to God. He lived among the people of the Sahara, and died at the hand of an assassin during an uprising against the French. His words echo those of Jesus at his crucifixion, as recorded in Luke 24:46.

Father, I abandon myself into your hands;
do with me what you will.
Whatever you do I thank you.
I am ready for all, I accept all.
Let only your will be done in me,
as in all your creatures,
I ask no more than this, my Lord.

Into your hands I commend my soul;
I offer it to you, O Lord,
with all the love of my heart,
for I love you, my God, and so need to give myself,
to surrender myself into your hands,
without reserve and with total confidence,
for you are my Father.

Charles de Foucauld (1858–1916)

Accept our sacrifice

Thomas Cranmer came to prominence at the time when Henry VIII was seeking the annulment of his first marriage, to Catherine of Aragon, to enable him to marry Anne Boleyn. Thomas was later appointed Archbishop of Canterbury and Henry both respected and protected him. He was the main compiler of the first Book of Common Prayer (1549 and 1552), from which this prayer below is taken. Cranmer was involved in church reform under Edward VI but under the Catholic Mary Tudor he was burnt at the stake. This was ordered despite the fact that, under extreme pressure, he had signed a document recanting his Protestantism. He was expected to do this again publicly at his execution but instead he reaffirmed his Protestant convictions and at the stake he held his right hand (with which he had signed the recantation) in the flames. His martyr's death, following those of Latimer and Ridley, did much to win people to Protestantism.

O Lord and heavenly Father, we thy humble servants entirely desire thy fatherly goodness mercifully to accept this our sacrifice of praise and thanksgiving; most humbly beseeching thee to grant, that by the merits and death of thy Son Jesus Christ, and through faith in his blood, we and all thy whole Church may obtain remission of our sins, and all other benefits of his passion. And here we offer and present unto thee, O Lord, ourselves, our souls and bodies, to be a reasonable, holy, and lively sacrifice unto thee; humbly beseeching thee, that all we, who are partakers of this holy Communion, may be fulfilled with thy grace and heavenly benediction. And although we be unworthy, through our manifold sins, to offer unto thee any sacrifice, yet we beseech thee to accept this our bounden duty and service; not weighing our merits, but pardoning our offences, through Jesus Christ our Lord; by whom, and with whom, in the unity of the Holy Ghost, all honour and glory be unto thee, O Father Almighty, world without end. Amen.

Thomas Cranmer (1489–1556)

All manner of thing shall be well

Julian of Norwich was one of the great English mystics. Little is known about her life except her writings. She is called Julian of Norwich simply because she lived in a cell adjoining the Benedictine church of St Julian in Conisford, Norwich. Having narrowly survived death from illness at the age of 30 (purportedly through prayer) she fell seriously ill once more in 1373 and experienced a series of 16 revelatory visions, mostly concerning the passion of Christ. After her recovery she meditated on these visions and went on to record her thoughts.

And thus, in my folly, afore this time often I wondered why, by the great foreseeing wisdom of God, the beginning of sin was not stopped; for then, I, all should have been well. ... But Jesus, who in this Vision informed me of all that is needful to me, answered by this word and said, Sin is unavoidable, but all shall be well, and all shall be well, and all manner of thing shall be well.

For if we never fell, we should not know how feeble and how wretched we are of our self, and also we should not fully know that marvellous love of our Maker.

The fullness of Joy is to behold God in everything.

God is all that is good, in my sight, and the goodness that everything has is his.

If there be anywhere on earth where a lover of God is always kept safe from falling, I know nothing of it, for it was not shown me. But this was shown: that in falling and rising again we are always kept in the same precious love.

Between God and the soul there is no between.

He did not say, You will never have a rough passage, you will never be over-strained, you will never feel uncomfortable, but he did say You will never be overcome.

Julian of Norwich (c. 1342–c. 1416) Revelations of Divine Love

All other love

The love of Christ surpasses all earthly love, and only love that originates with God has any permanence – this is the message of an anonymous fourteenth-century poet.

All other love is like the moon
That waxeth or waneth as flower in plain
As flower that blooms and fadeth soon,
As day that showereth and ends in rain.

All other love begins with bliss,
In weeping and woe makes its ending;
No love there is that's our whole bliss
But that which rests on heaven's king.

Anon. (c. 1350)

Alleluia

Born in present-day Algeria, Augustine was educated in North Africa and went on to become a bishop in the church there. His works, including the autobiographical Confessions, *are still widely read. This particular saying has a timeless quality.*

A Christian should be an alleluia from head to foot.

St Augustine of Hippo (354–430)

All-knowing God

In this psalm, the writer reflects on the fact that God has always known about him and is with him in every circumstance, having planned his life before it even began.

O LORD, you have searched me and known me.
You know when I sit down and when I rise up;
you discern my thoughts from far away.
You search out my path and my lying down,
and are acquainted with all my ways.
Even before a word is on my tongue,
O LORD, you know it completely.
You hem me in, behind and before,
and lay your hand upon me.
Such knowledge is too wonderful for me;
it is so high that I cannot attain it.

Where can I go from your spirit?
Or where can I flee from your presence?
If I ascend to heaven, you are there;
if I make my bed in Sheol, you are there.
If I take the wings of the morning
and settle at the farthest limits of the sea,
even there your hand shall lead me,
and your right hand shall hold me fast.
If I say, 'Surely the darkness shall cover me,
and the light around me become night',
even the darkness is not dark to you;
the night is as bright as the day,
for darkness is as light to you.

For it was you who formed my inward parts;
you knit me together in my mother's womb.
I praise you, for I am fearfully and wonderfully made.
Wonderful are your works;
that I know very well.
My frame was not hidden from you,
when I was being made in secret,
intricately woven in the depths of the earth.
Your eyes beheld my unformed substance.
In your book were written
all the days that were formed for me,
when none of them as yet existed.
How weighty to me are your thoughts, O God!
How vast is the sum of them!
I try to count them – they are more than the sand;
I come to the end – I am still with you.

O that you would kill the wicked, O God,
and that the bloodthirsty would depart from me –
those who speak of you maliciously,
and lift themselves up against you for evil!
Do I not hate those who hate you, O LORD?
And do I not loathe those who rise up against you?
I hate them with perfect hatred;
I count them my enemies.
Search me, O God, and know my heart;
test me and know my thoughts.
See if there is any wicked way in me,
and lead me in the way everlasting.

Psalm 139, NRSV

Amazing grace

John Newton had worked for a slave-owner and had himself been in chains after attempting to desert from his ship. He went on to become a slave-ship captain but was converted to evangelical Christianity in 1748 after his ship almost sank in a storm. Later in life he renounced the slave trade, and became a clergyman. He supported William Wilberforce in his work to abolish slavery.

Amazing grace, how sweet the sound
That saved a wretch like me!
I once was lost, but now am found,
Was blind, but now I see.

'Twas grace that taught my heart to fear,
And grace my fears relieved;
How precious did that grace appear,
The hour I first believed!

Through many dangers, toils and snares,
I have already come;
'Tis grace has brought me safe thus far,
And grace will lead me home.

The Lord has promised good to me,
His word my hope secures;
He will my shield and portion be,
As long as life endures.

Yes, when this flesh and heart shall fail,
And mortal life shall cease;
I shall possess, within the veil,
A life of joy and peace.

The earth shall soon dissolve like snow,
The sun forbear to shine;
But God, who called me here below,
Will be forever mine.

John Newton (1725–1807)

The apologist's evening prayer

Clive Staples Lewis was an Irish-born writer and scholar. An atheist from the age of fifteen he slowly returned to faith in his early thirties. He was a close friend and colleague of J R R Tolkein at Oxford, where he lived for many years. He wrote a number of books but is perhaps best known for The Chronicles of Narnia *books.*

From all my lame defeats and oh! much more
From all the victories that I seem to score;
From cleverness shot forth on thy behalf
At which, while angels weep, the audience laugh;
From all my proofs of thy divinity
Thou, who wouldst give no other sign, deliver me

Thoughts are but coins. Let me not trust instead
Of thee, their thin-worn image of my head.
From all me thoughts, even from my thoughts of thee
O thou fair Silence, fall, and set me free.
Lord of the narrow gate and the needle's eye,
Take me from all my trumpery lest I die.

C S Lewis (1898–1963)

As the sun sets

St Basil the Great describes how early Christians, rather than taking the light of lamps for granted, would thank God for it using the words of this ancient hymn, which is believed to date from the second century.

Now, as the sun sets in the west,
Soft lamplight glows as evening starts;
Thus, light from light, God's Son all blest
Comes from the immortal Father's heart.

We therefore sing our joyful songs
To Father, Holy Spirit, Son,
To whom in every age belongs
By right all praise from every tongue.

Lord Jesus, Son of God, from you
All life, all joy come forth this night;
The world, and each soft glowing hue,
Reflect the glory of your light.

Anon. (2nd century)

Ask and you will receive

Jesus taught that those who seek God will find answers and direction. He also assured his followers that faithful prayer will be answered.

'Ask, and it will be given to you; search, and you will find; knock, and the door will be opened for you. For everyone who asks receives, and everyone who searches finds, and for everyone who knocks, the door will be opened.'

Whatever you ask for in prayer with faith, you will receive.
Matthew 7:7–8; 21:22, NRSV

Ask God for wisdom

James writes to the early church, stressing the importance of a life lived in devotion to God. Believing in the right things is not enough – followers of Jesus must also live according to their faith. But this is no easy task and James reassures his readers that help is available.

If any of you is lacking in wisdom, ask God, who gives to all generously and ungrudgingly, and it will be given you. But ask in faith, never doubting, for the one who doubts is like a wave of the sea, driven and tossed by the wind.
James 1:5–6, NRSV

At Christmas

Although he came from a moderately well-off family, Charles Dickens
worked in a factory from the age of 12 and the dreadful conditions had an
impact on him that shaped his social conscience; the conditions under which
working-class people lived became major themes of his writing. One of his
best known novels is A Christmas Carol, *from which this extract is taken.*

For it is good to be children sometimes, and never better
than at Christmas, when its mighty Founder was a child himself.

Charles Dickens (1812–1870)

At the beginning of the day

Taken from the Book of Common Prayer, *this prayer seeks the*
protection of God for the day ahead. It is used in the shorter form of the
service of Morning Prayer.

O Lord, our heavenly Father, Almighty and everlasting God,
who hast safely brought us to the beginning of this day; Defend
us in the same with thy mighty power; and grant that this day we
fall into no sin, neither run into any kind of danger; but that all
our doings, being ordered by thy governance, may be righteous
in thy sight; through Jesus Christ our Lord. Amen.

The Book of Common Prayer

At your side

The book of Proverbs contains many two-line pieces of wisdom. Some of these have become everyday sayings or proverbs that are still in use today. This reminds us that as friends or as family members we should be faithful, loving and supportive.

A friend loves at all times, and kinsfolk are born to share adversity.

Proverbs 17:17, NRSV

Be of good cheer

The nineteenth-century preacher Robert Murray McCheyne died young but had made a significant impact in his seven years of ministry in Scotland. Here he writes to his church about suffering.

God has called you to suffer, and you go, like Abraham, not knowing whither you go ... Still, be of good cheer, suffer with Christ! God marks your every step ... He that loves you with an infinite, unchanging love, is leading you by his Spirit and providence. He knows every stone, every thorn in your path.

Robert Murray McCheyne (1813–1843)

Be prepared for trials

Maximilian Kolbe was a Polish Franciscan friar. He founded a monastery in Japan during the 1930s and during the Second World War he sheltered Polish refugees, many of them Jewish. He was arrested by the Gestapo and imprisoned in Auschwitz. In July 1941, ten men from his barracks were selected to be starved to death and Maximilian volunteered to take the place of one of them. After three weeks of dehydration and starvation, Kolbe and three others were still alive and he was finally murdered with an injection of carbolic acid. He is one of ten twentieth-century martyrs depicted above the Great Door of Westminster Abbey in London.

You must be prepared for periods of darkness, anxiety, doubts, fears, of temptations that are sometimes very, very insistent, of sufferings of the body and, what is a hundred times more painful, of the soul. For if there were nothing to bear, for what would you go to heaven? If there were no trials, there would be no struggle. Without a struggle, victory would be impossible, and without victory, there is no crown, no reward ... So be prepared from now on for everything.

Maximilian Kolbe (1894–1941)

Beauty

Clement, a Greek philosopher, united the traditions of Greek philosophy with Christian doctrine. Origen was his pupil in Alexandria and went on to become a renowned theologian.

It is not your outward appearance that you should beautify, but your soul, adorning it with good works. Although the body, to be precise, should be made beautiful, though in a measured way.

Clement of Alexandria (c. 150–c. 215)

Being born again

Jesus taught his followers that being 'born again' was necessary for those who wanted to be part of God's kingdom. When asked about how this could happen, his reply makes it clear that this new birth is a radical change brought about by the Spirit of God in the inner being.

Now there was a Pharisee named Nicodemus, a leader of the Jews. He came to Jesus by night and said to him, 'Rabbi, we know that you are a teacher who has come from God; for no one can do these signs that you do apart from the presence of God.' Jesus answered him, 'Very truly, I tell you, no one can see the kingdom of God without being born from above.' Nicodemus said to him, 'How can anyone be born after having grown old? Can one enter a second time into the mother's womb and be born?' Jesus answered, 'Very truly, I tell you, no one can enter the kingdom of God without being born of water and Spirit. What is born of the flesh is flesh, and what is born of the Spirit is spirit. Do not be astonished that I said to you, "You must be born from above." The wind blows where it chooses, and you hear the sound of it, but you do not know where it comes from or where it goes. So it is with everyone who is born of the Spirit.'

John 3:1–8, NRSV

Being fruitful again

Christina Rossetti was a poet and sister of the artist Dante Gabriel Rossetti. Her Christmas poem 'In the Bleak Midwinter' became widely known after her death when it was set as a Christmas carol. In these lines from another poem she reflects on the fact that painful circumstances can be used to help us grow and develop.

Although today he prunes my twigs with pain,
Yet doth his blood nourish and warm my root;
Tomorrow I shall put forth buds again
And clothe myself with fruit.

Christina Rossetti (1830–1894)

Belief in the unseen

In a scientific age we can be tempted to want proof of everything. We believe only what we can see. Far from losing their faith in the unseen, those who have suffered for their faith down through the ages have often found strength and comfort. In Germany during the Second World War, Jews in hiding left this inscription on a cellar wall.

I believe in the sun even when it is not shining. I believe in love even when feeling it not. I believe in God even when he is silent.

Anon. (20th century)

The best things

Robert Louis Stevenson was born in Scotland, where both his father and his grandfather had been lighthouse keepers. He is best known as the author of Treasure Island. *He died in Samoa at the age of just 44.*

The best things are nearest: breath in your nostrils, light in your eyes, flowers at your feet, duties at your hand, the path of God just before you.

Robert Louis Stevenson (1850–1894)

Beware anxiety

Charles Haddon Spurgeon was an English Baptist preacher who became a pastor at the age of just seventeen. He also founded the charity organization now known as Spurgeon's, which works worldwide with families and children. His sermons were translated into many languages in his lifetime and are still read and quoted from today by Christians of all denominations.

Anxiety does not empty tomorrow of its sorrow – only today of its strength.

Charles Haddon Spurgeon (1834–1892)

Beyond our understanding

Origen is generally considered the greatest theologian and biblical scholar of the early Eastern church. He was probably born in Egypt, and was taught by Clement of Alexandria. Origen's literary productivity was enormous. His writings helped to create a Christian theology that blended biblical and philosophical study.

Of all the marvellous and splendid things about the Son of God there is one that utterly transcends the limits of human wonder and is beyond the capacity of our weak mortal intelligence to think of or understand, namely, how this mighty power of the divine majesty, the very Word of the Father, and the very Wisdom of God, in which were created 'all things visible and invisible', can be believed to have existed within the compass of that man who appeared in Judaea; yes, and how the wisdom of God can have entered into a woman's womb and been born as a child and uttered noises like those of crying children; and further, how it was that he was troubled, as we are told, in the hour of death, as he himself confesses when he says, 'My soul is sorrowful even unto death'; and how at the last he was led to that death which is considered by men to be the most shameful of all – even though on the third day he rose again.

Origen (c. 185–254)

The Bible is a vein of pure gold

Charles Haddon Spurgeon is remembered primarily for his preaching, although he is also known as the founder of Spurgeon's, the international charity working throughout the world with families and children. Here he expounds on what makes the Bible so special.

The Bible is a vein of pure gold, unalloyed by quartz or any earthly substance. This is a star without a speck, a sun with a blot, a light without darkness, a moon without its paleness, and a glory without a dimness. O Bible! It cannot be said of any other book that it is perfect and pure, but of the Bible we can declare that all wisdom is gathered up in it without a particle of folly. This is the judge that ends the strife where wit and reason fail. This is the book untainted by any error; but is pure, unalloyed, perfect truth.

Charles Haddon Spurgeon (1834–1892)

Bless our meal

Martin Luther was a German monk and church reformer. Scripture was extremely important to him and his ideas were central to the Protestant Reformation.

Come, Lord Jesus, be our guest,
And may our meal by you be blest. Amen.
Attributed to Martin Luther (1483–1546)

Blessed are they ...

The passage in Matthew's Gospel known as the Beatitudes is part of Jesus'
teaching to his disciples in the Sermon on the Mount. Jesus declares the
blessings that come on those who live according to the distinctive principles of
the kingdom of God.

'Blessed are the poor in spirit, for theirs is the kingdom of
heaven.

Blessed are those who mourn, for they will be comforted.

Blessed are the meek, for they will inherit the earth.

Blessed are those who hunger and thirst for righteousness, for
they will be filled.

Blessed are the merciful, for they will receive mercy.

Blessed are the pure in heart, for they will see God.

Blessed are the peacemakers, for they will be called children
of God.

Blessed are those who are persecuted for righteousness' sake,
for theirs is the kingdom of heaven.

Blessed are you when people revile you and persecute you
and utter all kinds of evil against you falsely on my account.
Rejoice and be glad, for your reward is great in heaven, for in
the same way they persecuted the prophets who were before
you.'

Matthew 5:3–12, NRSV

A blessing

This blessing prayer, one of the best-known prayers and a particular favourite for christenings and other church services, is often known as the Aaronic blessing. It is based on the blessing that God gave to Moses for Aaron and the other priests to use to proclaim God's blessing to the Israelites.

The LORD bless you and keep you; the LORD make his face to shine upon you, and be gracious to you; the LORD lift up his countenance upon you and give you peace.

Numbers 6:24–26, NRSV

Blessing and honour

Lancelot Andrewes was an English clergyman and scholar who served as Bishop of Chichester during the reign of James I. He oversaw the translation of the King James Version of the Bible.

Blessing and honour, thanksgiving and praise
　　More than we can utter,
More than we can conceive,
Be unto you , O most holy and glorious Trinity,
　　Father, Son and Holy Spirit,
By all angels, all people, all creatures
　　For ever and ever. Amen and Amen.

Lancelot Andrewes (1555–1626)

The blessings of home and children

The psalmist reminds us that we need to ensure that God is involved in all that we do, or what we do will be fruitless. He also proclaims the benefits of having children.

Unless the LORD builds the house,
those who build it labour in vain.
Unless the LORD guards the city,
the guard keeps watch in vain.
It is in vain that you rise up early
and go late to rest,
eating the bread of anxious toil;
for he gives sleep to his beloved.

Sons are indeed a heritage from the LORD,
the fruit of the womb a reward.
Like arrows in the hand of a warrior
are the sons of one's youth.
Happy is the man who has
his quiver full of them.
He shall not be put to shame
when he speaks with his enemies in the gate.

Psalm 127, NRSV

Bound in this bundle of life

Reinhold Niebuhr was an American theologian, best known for trying to relate the Christian faith to the reality of twentieth-century politics. He contributed to modern thinking on the theory of the just war.

O God, who hast bound us together in this bundle of life, give us grace to understand how our lives depend upon the courage, the industry, the honesty and the integrity of our fellow-men; that we may be mindful of their needs, grateful for their faithfulness, and faithful in our responsibilities to them; through Jesus Christ our Lord.

Reinhold Niebuhr (1892–1971)

The bright morning star

George Fox was born in seventeenth-century Puritan England and became the founder of the Quakers. Although sometimes viewed as a fiery public figure, his letters reveal him as a loving pastor calling people to a confident and full Christian life.

All dear Friends everywhere, who have no helper but the Lord, who is your strength and your life, let your cries and prayers be to him, who with his eternal power has kept your heads above all waters and storms. Let none go out of their habitations in the stormy time of the night, those whose habitation is the Lord, the Seed, Christ Jesus.

In this Seed you will see the bright and morning Star appear which will expel the night of darkness, by which morning Star you will come to the everlasting Day which was before night was.

So, everyone feel this bright morning Star in your hearts, there to expel the darkness.

George Fox (1624–1691)

Canticle of the Sun

Francis of Assisi began preaching in 1208 and received papal approval for the founding of his religious order in the following year. The last three years of his life were spent in solitude and prayer. He wrote a number of well-known prayers and poems, including the Canticle of the Sun.

Most high, all-powerful, all good, Lord! All praise is yours, all glory, all honour And all blessing.

To you alone, Most High, do they belong. No mortal lips are worthy To pronounce your name.

All praise be yours, my Lord, through all that you have made, And first my lord Brother Sun, Who brings the day; and light you give to us through him.

How beautiful is he, how radiant in all his splendour! Of you, Most High, he bears the likeness.

All praise be yours my Lord, through Brothers Wind and Air, And fair and stormy, all the weather's moods, By which you cherish all that you have made.

All praise be yours, my Lord, through Sister Water, So useful, lowly, precious and pure.

All praise be yours, my Lord, through Brother Fire, Through whom you brighten up the night. How beautiful is he, how gay! Full of power and strength.

All praise be yours my Lord, through Sister Earth, our mother Who feeds us in her sovereignty and produces Various fruits with coloured flowers and herbs.

All praise be yours, my Lord, through those who grant pardon. For love of you; through those who endure Sickness and trial.

Happy those who endure in peace, By you, Most High, they will be crowned.

All praise be yours, my Lord, through Sister Death, From whose embrace no mortal can escape. Woe to those who die in mortal sin! Happy those She finds doing your will! The second death can do no harm to them.

Praise and bless my Lord, and give him thanks, And serve him with great humility.

St Francis of Assisi (1181–1226)

Caring friendship

Henri Nouwen was a Dutch Catholic priest who wrote widely on the spiritual life. After teaching for many years he left America for Canada, where he lived as pastor in a community for men and women with learning disablities.

We tend to look at caring as an attitude of the strong toward the weak, of the powerful toward the powerless, of the haves toward the have-nots ... Still, when we honestly ask ourselves which persons in our lives mean the most to us, we often find that it is those who, instead of giving much advice, solutions, or cures, have chosen rather to share our pain and touch our wounds with a gentle and tender hand. The friend who can be silent with us in a moment of despair or confusion, who can stay with us in an hour of grief and bereavement, who can tolerate not-knowing, not-curing, not-healing and face with us the reality of our powerlessness, that is the friend who cares.

Henri Nouwen (1932–1996)

Children of God

In his letter to the Romans, the apostle Paul urged his readers to remember that, through their faith in Jesus Christ, they have been adopted into the family of God.

For all who are led by the Spirit of God are children of God. For you did not receive a spirit of slavery to fall back into fear, but you have received a spirit of adoption. When we cry, 'Abba! Father!' it is that very Spirit bearing witness with our spirit that we are children of God, and if children, then heirs, heirs of God and joint heirs with Christ – if, in fact, we suffer with him so that we may also be glorified with him.

Romans 8:14–17, NRSV

A chosen people

Peter's first letter was written to both Jewish and Gentile Christians scattered throughout Asia Minor, which approximates to modern-day Turkey. His words address all who feel alienated from the world around them or who suffer persecution – they are encouraged to remember what God has done for them and stand firm.

But you are a chosen race, a royal priesthood, a holy nation, God's own people, in order that you may proclaim the mighty acts of him who called you out of darkness into his marvellous light.

1 Peter 2:9, NRSV

Christ above everything

In his letter to the church at Colossae, the apostle Paul writes to counter the claims of a rival philosophy. Early in the letter he emphasizes the supremacy of Jesus Christ.

He is the image of the invisible God, the firstborn of all creation; for in him all things in heaven and on earth were created, things visible and invisible, whether thrones or dominions or rulers or powers – all things have been created through him and for him. He himself is before all things, and in all things hold together. He is the head of the body, the church; he is the beginning, the firstborn from the dead, so that he might come to have first place in everything.

Colossians 1:15–18, NRSV

Christ has the keys

Isaac Watts was an evangelical leader in the period following the Puritans. He is best remembered as a hymn-writer, and especially for his hymn 'When I survey the wondrous cross'.

Christ has the keys of death; and the gates of eternal life are in his keeping.

Isaac Watts (1647–1748)

Christ, the Lord, is risen today

Charles Wesley wrote over 8000 hymns. This triumphant hymn was written in 1739 for use at the first worship service at the Wesleyan Chapel in London; it is often sung at Easter, but may also be used at other times of the year.

Christ, the Lord, is risen today, Alleluia!
Sons of men and angels say, Alleluia!
Raise your joys and triumphs high, Alleluia!
Sing, ye heavens, and earth, reply, Alleluia!

Love's redeeming work is done, Alleluia!
Fought the fight, the battle won, Alleluia!
Lo! the Sun's eclipse is over, Alleluia!
Lo! he sets in blood no more, Alleluia!

Vain the stone, the watch, the seal, Alleluia!
Christ hath burst the gates of hell, Alleluia!
Death in vain forbids his rise, Alleluia!
Christ hath opened paradise, Alleluia!

Lives again our glorious King, Alleluia!
Where, O death, is now thy sting? Alleluia!
Once he died our souls to save, Alleluia!
Where thy victory, O grave? Alleluia!

Soar we now where Christ hath led, Alleluia!
Following our exalted Head, Alleluia!
Made like him, like him we rise, Alleluia!
Ours the cross, the grave, the skies, Alleluia!

Hail, the Lord of earth and heaven, Alleluia!
Praise to thee by both be given, Alleluia!
Thee we greet triumphant now, Alleluia!
Hail, the resurrection, thou, Alleluia!

King of glory, Soul of bliss, Alleluia!
Everlasting life is this, Alleluia!
Thee to know, thy power to prove, Alleluia!
Thus to sing and thus to love, Alleluia!

Hymns of praise then let us sing, Alleluia!
Unto Christ, our heavenly King, Alleluia!
Who endured the cross and grave, Alleluia!
Sinners to redeem and save. Alleluia!

But the pains that he endured, Alleluia!
Our salvation have procured, Alleluia!
Now above the sky he's King, Alleluia!
Where the angels ever sing. Alleluia!

Jesus Christ is risen today, Alleluia!
Our triumphant holy day, Alleluia!
Who did once upon the cross, Alleluia!
Suffer to redeem our loss. Alleluia!

Charles Wesley (1707–1788)

Christian humility

The writings of Jeremy Taylor, chaplain to the Archbishop of Canterbury William Laud, contain what is possibly the best commendation of Christian humility.

Humility is the great ornament and jewel of the Christian religion ... first put into a discipline and made a part of a religion by our Lord Jesus Christ ... Remember that the blessed Saviour of the world hath done more to prescribe, and transmit, and secure this grace, than any other; his whole life being a great continued example of humility, a vast descent from the glorious bosom of his Father, to the womb of a poor maiden, to the form of a servant, to the miseries of a sinner, to a life of labour, to a state of poverty, to a death of malefactors, to the grave of death, and to the intolerable calamities which we deserved.

Jeremy Taylor (1613–1667)

A Christmas prayer

Henri Nouwen was a Dutch Catholic priest who wrote widely on the spiritual life. After teaching for many years he left America for Canada, where he spent the last twelve years of his life at L'Arche community. It was here that many of his books were written.

O Lord, how hard it is to accept your way. You come to me as a small, powerless child born away from home. You live for me as a stranger in your own land. You die for me as a criminal outside the walls of the city, rejected by your own people, misunderstood by your friends, and feeling abandoned by your God.

As I prepare to celebrate your birth, I am trying to feel loved, accepted, and at home in this world, and I am trying to overcome the feelings of alienation and separation which continue to assail me. But I wonder now if my deep sense of homelessness does not bring me closer to you than my occasional feelings of belonging. Where do I truly celebrate your birth: in a cosy home or in an unfamiliar house, among welcoming friends or among unknown strangers, with feelings of well-being or with feelings of loneliness?

I do not have to run away from those experiences that are closest to yours. Just as you do not belong to this world, so I do not belong to this world. Every time I feel this way I have an occasion to be grateful and to embrace you better and taste more fully your joy and peace.

Come, Lord Jesus, and be with me where I feel poorest. I trust that this is the place where you will find your manger and bring your light. Come, Lord Jesus, come. Amen.

Henri Nouwen (1932–1996)

Christ's ladder to heaven

Herbert Hensley Henson was bishop of both Hereford and Durham in the first half of the twentieth century. He spoke out on national and international affairs, protesting about what he saw as Britain's appeasement when Mussolini invaded Abyssinia in the 1930s and condemning the anti-semitic policies of Nazi Germany. In this sermon extract he likens Communion to the ladder seen by Jacob in Genesis, reaching up to heaven and providing access to God.

The Holy Communion is Christ's ladder set up on the earth, whose top reaches to heaven. Thereby we ascend to God through him, for through him we have our access in one Spirit unto the Father. The patriarch's dream revealed what actually had been in existence all the while, though he knew it not. Holy Communion protests to us the unsuspected sanctity of common life, and bids us know the nearness of God. That is the central and vitalising reality of sacramental worship. All else is picture, and parable, and vesture of truth. Words, gestures, the 'creatures of Bread and Wine', have their worth and meaning as tokens and pledges of a spiritual fact, that 'in him we live and move and have our being', that 'we are Christ's and Christ is God's'. Therefore on the threshold of Holy Communion the words of the Gospel come to us with direct and luminous relevance: 'Let not your heart be troubled: ye believe in God, believe also in me.'

Herbert Hensley Henson (1863–1947)

Christ's second coming

Aiden Wilson Tozer was an American Protestant pastor best known as the author of many books. Among them at least two, The Pursuit of God *and* The Knowledge of the Holy, *are regarded as Christian classics. His books stress the possibility of and need for a deeper relationship with God. This extract is from* Who Put Jesus on the Cross?

The people of God, Christians who are living between the two mighty events of Christ's incarnation and his promised second coming, are not living in a vacuum.

It is amazing that segments in the Christian church that deny the possibility of the imminent return of the Lord Jesus accuse those who do believe in his soon coming of sitting around, twiddling their thumbs, looking at the sky, and blankly hoping for the best!

Nothing could be further from the truth. We live in the interim between his two appearances, but we do not live in a vacuum. We have much to do and little time in which to get it done!

A W Tozer (1897–1963)

The church

Charles Morrison was a British journalist and biographer. His famous saying about the church summarizes the paradox that the church consists of those who, in order to follow Christ, have first to acknowledge their own sin and therefore their unworthiness to be his followers.

The Church is a society of sinners – the only society in the world in which membership is based upon the single qualification that the candidate shall be unworthy of membership.

Charles C Morrison (1838–1923)

Church music

Music is an important part of almost all Christian church services, but while we strive for excellence in all things it is well to remember why we have music in church.

Church music should not be for entertainment, but a worship experience that lifts us to the portals of heaven and leaves us thinking of the greatness and goodness of God.

Alice Tucker

Circumstances

Arthur Pink was an evangelist and Christian scholar who became a Christian in his early twenties. He emigrated to America and pastored churches in a number of states. In 1934 he returned to England and turned to writing, but his work reached a wide audience only after his death when many of his writings were republished.

Faith is not occupied with difficulties, but with him with whom all things are possible. Faith is not occupied with circumstances, but with the God of circumstances.

A W Pink (1886–1952)

Comfort for bereaved parents

The German monk and church reformer Martin Luther wrote to a father following the sudden death of his son who had travelled to Wittenberg to study.

It is only natural that your son's death and the report of it should distress and grieve you and your dear wife, his parents. I do not blame you for this, for all of us, and I in particular, are stricken with sorrow. Yet I admonish you that you should much rather thank God for giving you such a good, pious son and for deeming you worthy of all the pains and money you have invested in him. But let this be your best comfort, as it is ours, that he fell asleep (rather than departed) decently and softly with such a fine testimony of his faith on his lips that we all marvelled. There can be as little doubt that he is with God, his true Father, in eternal blessedness, as there can be doubt that the Christian faith is true. Such a beautiful end as his cannot fail to lead heavenward.

Martin Luther (1483–1546)

Confessing our helplessness

F B Meyer was a Baptist minister with a wide teaching ministry that included the Keswick convention. He wrote many books, and is especially remembered for his devotional biographies. This extract comes from his book on Joshua.

We sometimes feel lonely and discouraged. The hosts with which we are accustomed to cooperate are resting quietly in their tents. No one seems able to enter our anxieties and plans. Our Jerichos are so formidable – the neglected parish, the empty church, the hardened congregation, the godless household. How can we ever capture these, and hand them over to the Lord, like dismantled castles, for him to occupy?

In our hours of disappointment, when we have tried our best in vain, and have fallen, it is good to go out alone, confessing our helplessness, and waiting for the vision, for then we shall be likeliest to see the Captain of the Lord's host. He will undertake our cause; he will marshal his troops and win the day. He will fling the walls of Jericho the ground. These walls can only fall down by faith, for faith allies itself with God's almighty hand, and becomes the channel along which the power of God can pass. Our cooperation may be required but only to walk around the walls, in priestly purity, and blowing the rams' horns.

F B Meyer (1847–1929)

Confession

Lancelot Andrewes was an English clergyman and scholar who served as Bishop of Chichester during the reign of James I. This prayer reminds us that we need to admit before God our faults and sins before we can know his forgiveness and cleansing.

Lord,
as we add day to day,
so sin to sin.
The just falleth seven times a day;
and I, an exceeding sinner,
seventy times seven;
a wonderful, a horrible thing, O Lord.
But I turn with groans
from my evil ways,
and I return into my heart,
and with all my heart I turn to thee,
O God of penitents and Saviour of sinners;
and evening by evening I will return
in the innermost marrow of my soul;
and my soul out of the deep
crieth unto thee.
I have sinned, O Lord, against thee,
heavily against thee;
alas, alas, woe is me! for my misery.
I repent, O me! I repent, spare me, O Lord,
I repent, O me, I repent,
help thou my impenitence.
Be appeased, spare me, O Lord;
be appeased, have mercy on me;
I said, Lord, have mercy upon me,
heal my soul, for I have sinned against thee.
Have mercy upon me, O Lord,
after Thy great goodness,
according to the multitude of thy mercies
do away mine offences.
Remit the guilt,
heal the wound,
blot out the stains,

clear away the shame,
rescue from the tyranny,
and make me not a public example.
O bring thou me out of my trouble,
cleanse thou me from secret faults,
keep back thy servant also from presumptuous sins.
My wanderings of mind and idle talking
lay not to my charge.
Remove the dark and muddy flood
of foul and wicked thoughts.
O Lord, I have destroyed myself;
whatever I have done amiss, pardon mercifully.
Deal not with us after our sins,
neither reward us after our iniquities.
Look mercifully upon our infirmities;
and for the glory of thy all-holy Name,
turn from us all those ills and miseries,
which by our sins, and by us through them,
are most righteously and worthily deserved.

Lancelot Andrewes (1555–1626)

Confidence in Christ

Ulrich Zwingli was a Swiss pastor. He narrowly escaped death after contracting plague in 1519. He was a scholar and in his writings he spoke out against corruption in the church; he was in favour of clerics being allowed to marry. He stands alongside Martin Luther and John Calvin as a leader of the Reformation.

Our confidence in Christ does not make us lazy, negligent or careless, but on the contrary it awakens us, urges us on, and makes us active in living righteous lives and doing good. There is no self-confidence to compare with this.

Ulrich Zwingli (1484–1531)

Conversion

The German monk and church reformer Martin Luther declared that salvation was only available through faith in Jesus Christ as the Messiah and that this faith did not require mediation by the church. Scripture was extremely important to him and his ideas were central to the Protestant Reformation.

When I am baptised or converted by the gospel, the Holy Spirit is present. He takes me as clay and makes of me a new creature, which is endowed with a different mind, heart, and thoughts, that is, with a true knowledge of God and a sincere trust in God's grace ... The very essence of my heart is renewed and changed.

Martin Luther (1483–1546)

Conversion to Christ

In a striking modern parallel to the story of the conversion of Saul, Sundar Singh tells how he too had been very opposed to the gospel yet experienced the presence of Jesus. Sundar Singh's reported experiences during the remainder of his short life have proved controversial, but he remains one of the permanently significant figures of Indian Christianity. He made it clear that Christianity is not an imported, alien, foreign religion but that it is indigenous to Indian needs, aspirations and faith.

Then as I prayed and looked into the light, I saw the form of the Lord Jesus Christ. It had such an appearance of glory and love. If it had been some Hindu incarnation I would have prostrated myself before it. But it was the Lord Jesus Christ whom I had been insulting a few days before. I felt that a vision like this could not come out of my own imagination. I heard a voice saying in Hindustani, 'How long will you persecute me? I have come to save you; you were praying to know the right way. Why do you not take it?' The thought then came to me, 'Jesus Christ is not dead but living and it must be He Himself.' So I fell at His feet and got this wonderful Peace which I could not get anywhere else. This is the joy I was wishing to get. When I got up, the vision had all but disappeared, but although the vision disappeared the Peace and joy have remained with me ever since.

Sundar Singh (1899–c. 1929)

Conviction of sin

Paul Tournier was a Swiss doctor and author who investigated the relationship between medicine, counselling and spiritual values. Although he did consider giving up medicine for counselling he finally decided to combine the two, and in 1937 he transformed his private medical practice into a counselling practice.

Many people confuse the conviction of sin with such feelings as inferiority, lack of self-confidence and so on. Yet whoever observes people closely can see that these feelings and the conviction of sin are not only different from each other but in certain regards are mutually exclusive.

A diffuse and vague guilt feeling kills the personality, whereas the conviction of sin gives life to the personality. The former depends on people, on public opinion, while the latter depends on God.

Paul Tournier (1898–1986)

Courage

Clive Staples Lewis was an Irish-born writer and scholar. An atheist from the age of fifteen he slowly returned to faith in his early thirties. He was a close friend and colleague of J R R Tolkein at Oxford and wrote a number of books but is perhaps best known for The Chronicles of Narnia *books. This brief quotation reminds us that we need to take risks and act on what we know we have to do.*

Courage is not simply one of the virtues, but the form of every virtue at the testing point, which means at the point of highest reality.

C S Lewis (1898–1963)

Covenant with God

On the second Sunday of each year Methodists across the UK celebrate their annual covenant service. At the heart of this service are said the following words, with which the congregation reaffirm their willingness to be used in God's service, not just in public and visible ways but in daily acts of service.

I am no longer my own, but yours.
Put me to what you will, rank me with whom you will;
Put me to doing, put me to suffering;
Let me be employed for you, or laid aside for you;
Let me be exalted for you, or brought low for you;
Let me be full, let me be empty;
Let me have all things, let me have nothing;
I freely and wholeheartedly yield all things to your pleasure
    and disposal.
And now, O Glorious and blessed God, Father, Son and
    Holy Spirit,
You are mine and I am yours.
So be it.
And the covenant which I have made on earth,
Let it be ratified in heaven.
Amen.

John Wesley (1703–1791)

The cross

Vittoria Colonna was an Italian noblewoman and poet. In this poem about the crucifixion of Christ she reminds us that his suffering served to wash us clean and give us peace from the guilt of our sin.

When writhe the Saviour's shoulders on the tree
And droops the holy body from the weight
Is there then no key to fit the gate
That heaven should not open for to see?
What grievous pangs he bore from sheer pity
Thus by his guiltless blood to recreate
Our spirits laved of all impurity!
Our surcease from war, within, wherever,
Comes from him, the author of our peace.
He is the sun whose brilliance blinds our eyes.
The Father's secrets, how will he release
To whom and where and when none can surmise.
Enough for us to know he cannot err.

Vittoria Colonna (1490–1547)

Crying to God

Saint Andrew of Crete, also known as Andrew of Jerusalem, was born in Damascus and entered the church at the age of fourteen. He rose to become archdeacon of the cathedral of Hagia Sophia in Constantinople (now Istanbul). Today he is mostly remembered as a great hymn-writer. These two verses, extracts from the hymn 'Whence shall my tears begin?' are part of an earnest prayer of confession and repentance.

Whence shall my tears begin?
What first-fruits shall I bear
Of earnest sorrow for my sin?
Or how my woes declare?
O thou! The merciful and gracious One,
Forgive the foul transgressions I have done.

I lie before thy door,
O turn me not away!
Nor in my old age give me o'er
To Satan for a prey!
But ere the end of life and term of grace,
Thou merciful, my many sins efface!

Andrew of Crete (c. 660–732)

Daily seeking after God

Richard Baxter was an English Puritan church leader and theologian. He is perhaps best known now for writing the hymn 'Ye Holy Angels Bright', written in the year of his wife's death. At the age of seventy he was imprisoned by the notorious Judge Jeffreys, but the years following his release, despite poor health, were his most productive. A devotional work, Call to the Unconverted to Turn and Live, *was apparently instrumental in the conversion of thousands of people.*

Keep me, O Lord, while I tarry on this earth,
In a daily serious seeking after thee,
And in a believing affectionate walking with thee,
That, when thou comest, we may be found
Not hiding our talent,
Nor serving the flesh,
Nor yet asleep with our lamp unfurnished;
But waiting and longing for our Lord,
Our glorious God for ever and ever.

Richard Baxter (1615–1691)

Dare to believe

This anonymous poem points the way to a realistic acceptance of our human limitations, but with an optimistic slant that encourages us to aim to be the best that we can be, using the abilities and talents that we have been given.

You can't be all things to all people.
You can't do all things at once.
You can't do all things equally well.
You can't do all things better than everyone else.
Your humanity is showing just like everyone else's.

So ...

You have to find out who you are, and be that.
You have to decide what comes first, and do that.
You have to discover your strengths, and use them.
You have to learn not to compete with others,
Because no one else is in the contest of 'being you'.

Then ...

You will have learned to accept your own uniqueness.
You will have learned to set priorities and make decisions.
You will have learned to live with your limitations.
You will have learned to give yourself the respect that is due,
And you'll be a being that's vitally alive.

Dare to believe ...

That you are a wonderful, unique person.
That you are a once-in-all-history event.
That it's more than a right, it's your duty, to be who you are.
That life is not a problem to solve, but a gift to cherish.
And you'll be able to stay one up on what used to get you
    down.

Anon.

Dedicating all to God

The following prayer appears in a collection of prayers for Methodist preachers. It is designed to be said as a responsive prayer, as a re-dedication to the task of discipleship by the congregation.

For the hallowing of daily life and common tasks in patience and faithfulness:
We offer ourselves to thee, O Lord.
For the adventure in untried ways, whithersoever thou dost lead:
We offer ourselves to thee, O Lord.
For the way of prayer and concern for others:
We offer ourselves to thee, O Lord.
For the way of fellowship and the bearing of others' burdens:
We offer ourselves to thee, O Lord.
For the way of loving and the winning of souls:
We offer ourselves to thee, O Lord.
For the way of sacrifice, withholding nothing, that we may do thy perfect will:
We offer ourselves to thee, O Lord.

Anon.

Delight in the Lord

This psalm shows us two ways to live: those who put into practice God's word are happy. They do not follow the ways of evildoers, but they enjoy his word, and they therefore stay fresh and lead fruitful lives for him.

Happy are those
who do not follow the advice of the wicked,
or take the path that sinners tread,
or sit in the seat of scoffers;
but their delight is in the law of the LORD,
and on his law they meditate day and night.
They are like trees
planted by streams of water,
which yield their fruit in its season,
and their leaves do not wither.
In all that they do, they prosper.

The wicked are not so,
but are like chaff that the wind drives away.
Therefore the wicked will not stand in the judgement,
nor sinners in the congregation of the righteous;
for the LORD watches over the way of the righteous,
but the way of the wicked will perish.

Psalm 1, NRSV

Deliver us from cold hearts

William Bright was an English church historian, priest and theologian. He became Professor of Ecclesiastical History and Canon of Christ Church, Oxford. He wrote a number of hymns and compiled an anthology of prayers.

O Almighty God, from whom every good prayer comes, and who pours out on all who desire it the spirit of grace and supplications: deliver us, when we draw near to you, from coldness of heart and wanderings of mind; that with steadfast thoughts and kindled affections we may worship you in spirit and in truth, through Christ Jesus our Lord.

William Bright (1824–1901)

Different gifts

Jeremy Taylor was a seventeenth-century bishop and writer. In this extract he illustrates how the Holy Spirit gives different gifts to the members of the church, as described by the apostle Paul in 1 Corinthians 12:4–11.

Mark the rain that falls from above; the same shower that drops out of one cloud increases sundry plants in a garden, and severally, according to the condition of every plant. In one stalk it makes a rose; in another a violet; diverse in a third; and sweet in all. So the Spirit works its many and varied effects in several complexions, and all according to the increase of God.

Jeremy Taylor (1613–1667)

Discipleship

Oswald Chambers was a prominent early-twentieth-century Scottish Christian minister and teacher, best known as the author of the widely read devotional My Utmost for His Highest. *He died in Egypt where he was serving as a chaplain during the First World War. He had developed appendicitis but, refusing to take a hospital bed needed for wounded soldiers, his appendix ruptured, with fatal consequences.*

Discipleship is built entirely on the supernatural grace of God. Walking on the water is easy to impulsive pluck, but walking on dry land as a disciple of Jesus Christ is a different thing. Peter walked on the water to go to Jesus, but he followed him afar off on the land. We do not need the grace of God to stand crisis, human nature and pride are sufficient, we can face the strain magnificently; but it does require the supernatural grace of God to live twenty-four hours in every day as a saint, to go through the drudgery as a disciple, to live an ordinary, unobserved, ignored existence as a disciple of Jesus. It is inbred in us that we have to do exceptional things for God; but we have not. We have to be exceptional in the ordinary things, to be holy in mean streets, among mean people, and this is not learned in five minutes.

Oswald Chambers (1874–1917)

Distractions

John Donne was a Jacobean poet and preacher, whose many works include sonnets, love poetry and religious poems. He came from a Roman Catholic family, and experienced persecution until his conversion to the Anglican Church. In this passage readers will recognize the difficulties of applying themselves to prayer – distractions that have changed very little since Donne wrote, over three hundred years ago.

When we consider with a religious seriousness the manifold weaknesses of the strongest devotions in time of prayer, it is a sad consideration. I throw myself down in my chamber, and I call in, and invite God, and his angels thither, and when they are there, I neglect God and his angels, for the noise of a fly, for the rattling of a coach, for the whining of a door; I talk on, in the same posture of praying, eyes lifted up, knees bowed down, as though I prayed to God; and, if God or his angels should ask me when I thought last of God in that prayer, I cannot tell: sometimes I find that I had forgot what I was about, but when I began to forget it, I cannot tell. A memory of yesterday's pleasures, a fear of tomorrow's dangers, a straw under my knee, a noise in mine ear, a light in mine eye, an anything, a nothing, a fancy, a chimera in my brain, troubles me in my prayer. So certainly is there nothing, nothing in spiritual things, perfect in this world.

John Donne (1572–1631)

Do not fear

In an extended passage of prophecy from the book of Isaiah which begins with the famous words, 'Comfort, O comfort my people, says your God' (Isaiah 40:1), the prophet reassures God's people Israel that their God is with them.

'do not fear, for I am with you,
do not be afraid, for I am your God;
I will strengthen you, I will help you,
I will uphold you with my victorious right hand.'

Isaiah 41:10, NRSV

Do not worry

In Jesus' best-known teaching, the Sermon on the Mount, which is reported in Matthew chapters 5 to 7, he includes many guidelines for right living. He also tells his followers that they should not be concerned about material things – they should look at creation and see how well their Father God takes care of what he has made.

Therefore I tell you, do not worry about your life, what you will eat or what you will drink, or about your body, what you will wear. Is not life more than food, and the body more than clothing? Look at the birds of the air; they neither sow nor reap nor gather into barns, and yet your heavenly Father feeds them. Are you not of more value than they? And can any of you by worrying add a single hour to your span of life? And why do you worry about clothing? Consider the lilies of the field, how they grow; they neither toil nor spin, yet I tell you, even Solomon in all his glory was not clothed like one of these. But if God so clothes the grass of the field, which is alive today and tomorrow is thrown into the oven, will he not much more clothe you – you of little faith? Therefore do not worry, saying, 'What will we eat?' or 'What will we drink?' or 'What will we wear?' For it is the Gentiles who strive for all these things; and indeed your heavenly Father knows that you need all these things. But strive first for the kingdom of God and his righteousness, and all these things will be given to you as well.

So do not worry about tomorrow, for tomorrow will bring worries of its own. Today's trouble is enough for today.

Matthew 6:25–34, NRSV

Doing good today

Stephen Grellet was born in France and during the French Revolution he was imprisoned but escaped to America. Raised as a Catholic, he became a Quaker and encouraged many reforms in educational policies and in hospital and prison conditions. This prayer reflects his concern that as Christians we should use our lives to make a difference.

Dear Lord Jesus, we shall have this day only once; before it is gone, help us to do all the good we can, so that today is not a wasted day.

Stephen Grellet (1773–1855)

The donkey

Gilbert Keith Chesterton, known by his initials, was an extremely prolific writer. He produced around eighty books, several hundred poems, some 200 short stories, 4000 essays and several plays. Here he puts himself in the place of the humble donkey, an animal that is often ridiculed but that was nevertheless given the honour of bearing Christ in triumph into Jerusalem on Palm Sunday.

When fishes flew and forests walked
And figs grew upon thorn,
Some moment when the moon was blood
Then surely I was born;

With monstrous head and sickening cry
And ears like errant wings,
The devil's walking parody
On all four-footed things.

The tattered outlaw of the earth,
Of ancient crooked will;
Starve, scourge, deride me: I am dumb,
I keep my secret still.

Fools! For I also had my hour;
One far fierce hour and sweet:
There was a shout about my ears,
And palms before my feet.

G K Chesterton (1874–1936)

Don't be afraid

Fyodor Dostoevsky was a nineteenth-century Russian novelist. He spent a number of years imprisoned in Siberia for being a member of a liberal intellectual group. He died in 1881 and his tombstone reads: 'Verily, Verily, I say unto you, Except a corn of wheat fall into the ground and die, it abideth alone: but if it die, it bringeth forth much fruit.' This is taken from John 12:24, and is also the epigraph of his final novel, The Brothers Karamazov.

Don't be afraid of anything. Do not ever be afraid. And don't worry. So long as you remain sincerely penitent, God will forgive you everything. There's no sin, and there can be no sin in the whole world which God will not forgive to those who are truly repentant. Why, no one can commit so great a sin as to exhaust the infinite love of God. Or can there be a sin that would exceed the love of God? Only you must never forget to think continually of repentance, but dismiss your fear altogether. Believe that God loves you in a way you cannot even conceive of. He loves you in spite of your sin and in your sin. And there's more joy in heaven over one sinner that repents than over ten righteous men. This was said a long time ago. So go and do not be afraid. Do not be upset by people and do not be angry if you are wronged ... if you are sorry for what you did, then you must love. And if you love, you are of God ... Everything can be atoned for, everything can be saved by love. If I, a sinner like you, have been moved by your story and am sorry for you, how much more will God be. Love is such a priceless treasure that you can redeem everything in the world by it, and expiate not only your own but other people's sins. Go and do not be afraid.

Fyodor Dostoevsky (1821–1881)

Dying daily

François Fénelon was a French Roman Catholic theologian, poet and writer. He was ordained in his early twenties and joined a religious Order. He became an advocate of Quietism, which emphasized intellectual stillness and interior passivity as essential conditions of perfection.

The greatest of all crosses is self – if we die in part every day, we shall have but little to do on the last. These little daily deaths will destroy the power of the final dying.

François Fénelon (1651–1715)

Dying well

Pope John XXIII was elected in 1958 and is especially remembered for calling the Second Vatican Council, which sat from 1962 to 1965. He did not live to see it complete its task, dying in 1963.

It is an indisputable truth that all of us one day will receive a visit from our sister Death, as Saint Francis of Assisi called her. She sometimes represents herself in a sudden and unexpected manner. But we shall remain tranquil, or better undisturbed, if our tree has known how to yield its fruits. He who has worked well, departs when the day is ended.

Pope John XXIII (1881–1963)

Easter

Desmond Tutu was a teacher in South Africa but went on to study theology after resigning in protest at the poor educational prospects for black South Africans. In 1975 he was appointed Dean of Johannesburg and was later elected and consecrated as the first ever black archbishop of Cape Town. He received the Nobel Peace Prize in 1984.

Easter means – hope prevails over despair. Jesus reigns as Lord of Lords and King of Kings ... Easter says to us that despite everything to the contrary, his will for us will prevail, love will prevail over hate, justice over injustice and oppression, peace over exploitation and bitterness.

Desmond Tutu (b. 1931)

Easter Day

Martin Manser is a reference-book editor and language trainer. He studied at the Universities of York, England and Regensburg, Germany and then undertook research into the influence of English on modern German. A developing interest in lexicography led him to take up a post as a reference-book editor. Since 1980 he has compiled or edited many reference books including titles that encourage Bible reading. He has also written a book of prayers, including this prayer that celebrates Christ's resurrection.

'I know that my Redeemer lives.'
Wow!
I worship you, Lord Jesus Christ, for this amazing fact that
    you came back to life and are alive right now.
That really is awesome!
Amidst all the questions I still have about life one certainty
    rings out to every point in the universe: Christ is risen!
The immortal One has died for all sin and for all sinners in
    every time and in every place.
Christ has been brought back to eternal life: surely this is the
    most thrilling victory of all time!
Lord Jesus Christ, you really are the Son of God.
I worship you in praise and adoration.
I give myself afresh to you right now on this day of all days.
Equip me with the power that raised Christ from the dead, to
    serve you today and all the days ahead.
In Christ's name, I pray. Amen.

Martin Manser (b. 1952)

Encouraging words

Cyprian was bishop of Carthage in North Africa from 249 until his death in 258. He refused to sacrifice to pagan deities and died a martyr at the hand of the Romans. His answer to the death sentence was, 'Thanks be to God!' Earlier, while imprisoned, he had written to some of his colleagues, imprisoned elsewhere, appealing for faith in the face of suffering and death.

What now must be the vigour, beloved brethren, of your victorious consciousness, what the loftiness of your mind, what exultation in feeling, what triumph in your breast, that every one of you stands near to the promised reward of God ... that you know Christ is present with you, rejoicing in the endurance of his servants, who are ascending by his footsteps and in his paths to the eternal kingdoms! You daily expect with joy the saving day of your departure; and already about to withdraw from the world, you are hastening to the rewards of martyrdom, and to the divine homes, to behold after this darkness of the world the purest light, and to receive a glory greater than all sufferings and conflicts, as the apostle witnesses, and says, 'The sufferings of this present time are not worthy to be compared with the glory that shall be revealed in us.' And because now your word is more effectual in prayers, and supplication is more quick to obtain what is sought for in afflictions, seek more eagerly, and ask that the divine condescension would consummate the confession of all of us; that from this darkness and these snares of the world God would set us also free with you, sound and glorious; that we who here are united in the bond of charity and peace, and have stood together against the wrongs of heretics and the oppressions of the heathens, may rejoice together in the heavenly kingdom. I bid you, most blessed and most beloved brethren, ever farewell in the Lord, and always and everywhere remember me.

Cyprian (c. 200–258)

The end of a pilgrimage

Christian pilgrimage began in the first few centuries of the early church. Today, many people still travel to holy places to seek a deepening of their faith. Having undertaken such a journey, the end of a pilgrimage marks a new beginning. The following prayer, written by Stephen Doyle, reflects on completing a pilgrimage to the Holy Land. Father Doyle, an American, teaches, writes and conducts retreats.

Father, we have walked in the land where Jesus walked.
We have touched the soil and rocks where the seed falls.
We have seen the lilies of the field and heard the birds of the
air.
We have been warmed by the sun that warmed him and
cooled by the breezes that touched his face.
We have been to the sea where he walked,
And to the river where he was baptised.
We have felt the presence of the Holy Spirit where he first
sent it, and anguished at the spot where he gave himself
for us.
We have rejoiced at the emptiness of the tomb and the
fullness of his love in our hearts.
Be with us, as we continue our earthly pilgrimage to the new
Jerusalem where every tear will be wiped away, and we
will be with you, your Son and the Holy Spirit forever.

Stephen Doyle OFM

Enlightenment faith

*Even as the development of science and reason led to a widespread
questioning of religious faith, there were those, among them the scientist and
philosopher Blaise Pascal, who nevertheless held both to scientific endeavour
and Christian faith. A brilliant mathematician, Pascal devoted the last eight
years of his short life to philosophy and theology.*

For after all what is man in nature? A nothing in relation to
infinity, all in relation to nothing, a central point between
nothing and all and infinitely far from understanding either. The
ends of things and their beginnings are impregnably concealed
from him in an impenetrable secret. He is equally incapable of
seeing the nothingness out of which he was drawn and the
infinite in which he is engulfed.

Blaise Pascal (1623–1662)

Epistle to Diognetus

The 'Epistle to Diognetus' was written by a second-century Christian to a pagan asking the simple question, 'What is a Christian?' The reply makes it clear that these early Christians were living lives of honesty, contentment, patience, love and kindness. It makes some challenging observations about the nature of Christian discipleship and ethics.

You cannot identify Christians from other people on the basis of nationality, language or customs.

They do not live in cities of their own, or speak some strange dialect, or adopt some peculiar lifestyle.

Their teaching is not the inventive speculation of inquisitive minds.

They are not propagating mere human teaching as some people do.

They live in Greek or foreign city, wherever chance has placed them.

They follow local customs in clothing, food and other aspects of life.

But at the same time they demonstrate the strangely wonderful form of their own citizenship.

They each live in their native land, but as strangers.

They shoulder all the duties of citizenship, but are made to suffer like aliens.

Every foreign country is to them a homeland, while every homeland is like a foreign country.

They marry and have children just like everyone else; but they do not kill unwanted babies.

They share a common table but not a common bed.

They are present 'in the flesh', but they do not live 'according to the flesh'.

They live upon earth, but they are citizens of heaven.

They obey human laws, but surpass these laws in their personal lives.

They love everyone, but are persecuted by all.

They are unknown, and yet they are condemned.

They are put to death and yet they are more alive than ever.

They are poor and yet make many rich.

They are short of everything and yet they live in abundance.

They are dishonoured and yet their dishonour becomes a
glory.

Their names are blackened; nevertheless they stand innocent.

They are mocked and yet they bless in return.

They are treated outrageously and yet behave respectfully to
all.

When they do good they are punished as evildoers.

When punished they rejoice as if being given new life.

They are attacked by Jews as aliens and persecuted by the
Greeks.

Yet those who hate them cannot give any reason for their
hostility.

To put it simply – life is to the body as Christians are to the
world.

Their life is in the body but is not of the body.

Christians are in the world but not of the world.

Life is locked into the body, yet it holds the body together.

Christians are held like prisoners in the world, yet it is they
that hold the world together.

Aristides (d. c. 134)

Evening prayer

John Baillie was a Scottish theologian and Church of Scotland minister. He wrote A Diary of Private Prayer, *published in 1936 and regarded as a devotional classic.*

Almighty God, in this hour of quiet I seek communion with thee. From the fret and fever of the day's business, from the world's discordant noises, from the praise and blame of men, from the confused thoughts and vain imaginations of my own heart, I would now turn aside and seek the quietness of thy presence. All day long I have toiled and striven; but now, in stillness of heart and in the clear light of thine eternity, I would ponder the pattern my life has been weaving.

... I am content, O Father, to leave my life in thy hands, believing that the very hairs upon my head are numbered by thee. I am content to give over my will to thy control, believing that I can find in thee a righteousness that I could never have won for myself. I am content to leave all my dear ones to thy care, believing that thy love for them is greater than my own. I am content to leave in thy hands the causes of truth and justice, and the coming of thy kingdom in the hearts on men, believing that my ardour for them is but a feeble shadow of thy purpose. To thee, O God, be glory for ever. Amen.

John Baillie (1886–1960)

An evening prayer

Born in present-day Algeria, Augustine was educated in North Africa and went on to become a bishop in the church there. He is known particularly for his autobiographical Confessions. *This prayer for the Lord's help and assurance at night is attributed to him.*

Keep watch, dear Lord,
With those who work, or watch, or weep this night;
And give your angels charge over those who sleep.
Tend the sick, give rest to the weary.
Sustain the dying, calm the suffering,
And pity the distressed;
All for your love's sake, O Christ our Redeemer.
Amen.

St Augustine of Hippo (354–430)

Expect great things

William Carey was from a poor background and had little education but after coming to faith as a teenager he served as a lay preacher, becoming fascinated by foreign lands and learning languages in order to read about them. He suggested the founding of a missionary society, and although initially opposed, his efforts eventually led to the founding of the Baptist Missionary Society. Carey served as its first missionary, in India, and translated the Bible into Bengali, Sanskrit and other languages.

Expect great things from God. Attempt great things for God.

William Carey (1761–1834)

Father, hear the prayer we offer

Love Maria Willis was the wife of a doctor who lived most of her life in Rochester, New York. Her poem, first published in about 1856, was revised for publication as a hymn in about 1884 and has remained popular. It contains a number of biblical allusions.

Father, hear the prayer we offer
Not for ease that prayer shall be
But for strength, that we may ever
Live our lives courageously.

Not for ever in green pastures
Do we ask our way to be
But by steep and rugged pathways
Would we strive to climb to thee.

Not for ever by still waters
Would we idly quiet stay
But would smite the living fountains
From the rocks along our way.

Be our strength in hours of weakness
In our wanderings be our Guide
Through endeavour, failure, danger
Father, be thou at our side.

Love Maria Willis (1824–1908)

The Father's dwelling-places

Jesus has washed the feet of his disciples and told them that one of them will betray him. He then explains to them that in having him with them they have seen the Father and know him, but that when he leaves, the Holy Spirit will come to them. His death will not be the end of their relationship with God.

'Do not let your hearts be troubled. Believe in God, believe also in me. In my Father's house there are many dwelling-places. If it were not so, would I have told you that I go to prepare a place for you? And if I go and prepare a place for you, I will come again and will take you to myself, so that where I am, there you may be also.'

John 14:1–3, NRSV

Following Jesus Christ

Jeremy Taylor was a seventeenth-century clergyman in the Church of England who achieved fame as an author during the Protectorate of Oliver Cromwell. He is known for his poetic style of writing. Following the restoration of the monarchy he was appointed as Bishop of Down and Connor.

Lord Jesus, come quickly; my heart is desirous of they presence, and would entertain thee, not as a guest, but as an inhabitant, as the Lord of my faculties. Enter in and take possession, and dwell with me for ever, that I also may dwell in the heart of my dearest Lord, which was opened for me with a spear and love. Amen.

Jeremy Taylor (1613–1667)

Food for all

The first Christian Aid week was held in 1957, organized by a body set up in the aftermath of the Second World War and originally called Christian Reconstruction in Europe. Their purpose was to alleviate suffering for ordinary people, no matter what their faith and they had already begun to look beyond Europe, to support development work in newly independent nations in Africa and Asia, and to respond to emergencies worldwide. In 1964 the organization changed its name to Christian Aid. Their current strapline is 'We believe in life before death'.

O God our Father, in the name of him who gave bread to the hungry we remember all who through our human ignorance, selfishness and sin are condemned to live in want; and we pray that all endeavours for the overcoming of world poverty and hunger may be so prospered that there may be found sufficient food for all; through Jesus Christ our Lord.

Christian Aid

Food for the faithful

Thomas Aquinas was born near Naples in Italy and joined the Dominican friars in his late teens. He studied in Paris and Cologne and helped the church to come to terms with the rediscovered philosophy of Aristotle. He maintained that this could be held together with Catholic theology and the resulting system of theology – known as Thomism – is still influential within the Catholic Church.

This food satisfies the hunger of the devout heart. Faith is the seasoning, devotion and love of the brethren the relish. The teeth of the body break this food, but only an unfaltering faith can savour it.

Thomas Aquinas (1225–1274)

For guidance

Patrick was a Christian missionary and is a patron saint of Ireland. He was born in Roman Britain. When he was about sixteen he was captured by Irish raiders and taken as a slave to Ireland, where he lived for six years before escaping and returning to his family. He entered the church, as his father and grandfather had done before him, becoming a deacon and a bishop. He later returned to Ireland as a missionary, working in the north and west of the island.

May the strength of God pilot us,
May the power of God preserve us,
May the wisdom of God instruct us,
May the hand of God protect us,
May the way of God direct us,
May the shield of God defend us,
May the host of God guard us against the snares of evil
And the temptations of the world.

St Patrick (c. 389–c. 461)

For the church

The following prayer for the church is of unknown origin but appears in a collection of prayers for Methodist preachers. It encompasses the work and purpose of the church and is a re-dedication to the task of discipleship on behalf of all who are part of the church.

O Lord, we beseech thee to maintain thy church in truth and patience; that her pastors may be faithful, her watchmen vigilant, her flock loyal, her camp united, her war spiritual, her weapons heavenly, her lamps burning and shining; and as thy Son Jesus Christ hath given so great a price for us, let us not count it a hard thing to give up all for him, and to spend and be spent for the souls he hath redeemed; through Jesus Christ our Lord. Amen.

Anon.

Forgetting myself

Michel Quoist is a French parish priest and theologian. He is best known for his devotional work Prayers of Life.

Lord, help me to forget myself for others, my brothers,
That in giving myself I may teach myself to love.

Michel Quoist (b. 1921)

Freedom from fear

H Elvet Lewis was a Welsh poet; he also wrote about the Welsh revival of 1904–1905 and co-wrote a book about lesser-known characters in the Bible.

Gracious Lord, grant that we may know sufficient about ourselves to feel afraid, and know enough about you to lose our fears. At the height of our temptations may we be fortified by your strength. Although we may often lose heart, let us not forget the Intercessor with the Father, Jesus Christ the righteous.

Give us a keen intellect to recognise his voice in every difficulty, on the steep hills and in the deep valleys where the darkness gathers. Lead us to the light: you are the Light. We were not meant to walk in darkness nor to live in fear. Neither the number of sorrowful nights nor the depth of the gloom shall be too much if in the end you bring us safely to the full noon of your love.

H Elvet Lewis (1860–1955)

Friendship

Jürgen Moltmann is a German Protestant theologian and author of many books. His experience as a prisoner of war between 1945 and 1948 gave him a great understanding of how suffering and hope reinforce each other, leaving a lasting impression on his theology. Here he writes in praise of friendship.

Friendship is no passing feeling of affection. It combines affection with faithfulness. You can depend upon a friend. As a friend you become someone upon whom others can depend. A friend remains a friend even in misfortune, even in guilt. For between friends there rules no prejudice that defines one, and no ideal image after which one must strive. Nor is friendship an alliance for mutual advantage, as is the case with so-called business friends. Between friends there rules only the promise to walk with each other and to be there for each other, in other words, a faithfulness that has to do not with acting and possessing, but with the individual person and with being.

Friendship is then a deep human relation that arises out of freedom, consists in mutual freedom, and preserves this freedom.

Jürgen Moltmann (b. 1926)

Friendship with God

Teresa Avila was born in Avila, Spain. In 1534, at the age of twenty, she entered the monastery of the Incarnation of the Carmelite nuns at Avila, where she often suffered from illness. In 1559, Teresa became firmly convinced that Christ was present to her in bodily form, though invisible. This vision lasted almost uninterruptedly for more than two years. She died in 1582, having founded a number of convents, and was canonized forty years after her death. In this passage she describes some of the benefits of prayer.

Anyone who has not begun to pray, I beg, for love of the Lord, not to miss so great a blessing. There is no place here for fear, but only desire. For, even if a person fails to make progress, or to strive after perfection, so that he may merit the consolations and favours given to the perfect by God, yet he will gradually gain a knowledge of the road to heaven. And if he perseveres, I hope in the mercy of God, whom no one has ever taken for a friend without being rewarded; and mental prayer, in my view, is nothing but friendly intercourse, and frequent solitary converse, with him whom we know loves us. If love is to be true and friendship lasting, certain conditions are necessary: on the Lord's side we know these cannot fail, but our nature is vicious, sensual and ungrateful. You cannot therefore succeed in loving him as much as he loves you, because it is not in your nature to do so. If, then, you do not yet love him, you will realise how much it means to you to have his friendship and how much he loves you, and you will gladly endure the troubles which arise from being so much with one who is so different from you.

Teresa of Avila (1515–1582)

Gain in godliness

In Paul's first letter to Timothy the apostle warns of the temptations that await those who want to become rich with worldly wealth. He reminds Timothy that none of this wealth lasts, only that which comes from faithfully following the ways of God.

Of course, there is great gain in godliness combined with contentment; for we brought nothing into the world, so that we can take nothing out of it; but if we have food and clothing, we will be content with these.

1 Timothy 6:6–8, NRSV

The gathered church

Gordon Fee is an American New Testament scholar and has written a number of books about studying the Bible. Here he reflects on what the church is.

The gathered church is the place of God's own personal presence, by the Spirit ... The local church is God's temple in the community where it is placed, and it is so by the presence of the Spirit alone, by whom God has now revisited his people.

Gordon Fee (b. 1926)

Gathered in God's granary

Bread and fish feature in a number of Gospel stories, notably the feeding of the multitudes and the breakfast on the lake shore after Jesus' resurrection. In this Irish prayer we are reminded that both bread and fish are the Lord's.

The seed is Christ's,
The granary is Christ's;
In the granary of God
May we be gathered.
The sea is Christ's,
The fishes are Christ's;
In the nets of God
May we all meet.

Irish prayer

The gift of love

In his first letter to the church at Corinth, the apostle Paul describes the characteristics of real love and how it surpasses all other spiritual gifts. This passage is frequently chosen for both weddings and funeral services.

If I speak in the tongues of mortals and of angels, but do not have love, I am a noisy gong or a clanging cymbal. And if I have prophetic powers, and understand all mysteries and all knowledge, and if I have all faith, so as to remove mountains, but do not have love, I am nothing. If I give away all my possessions, and if I hand over my body so that I may boast, but do not have love, I gain nothing.

Love is patient; love is kind; love is not envious or boastful or arrogant or rude. It does not insist on its own way; it is not irritable or resentful; it does not rejoice in wrongdoing, but rejoices in the truth. It bears all things, believes all things, hopes all things, endures all things.

Love never ends. But as for prophecies, they will come to an end; as for tongues, they will cease; as for knowledge, it will come to an end. For we know only in part, and we prophesy only in part; but when the complete comes, the partial will come to an end. When I was a child, I spoke like a child, I thought like a child, I reasoned like a child; when I became an adult, I put an end to childish ways. For now we see in a mirror, dimly, but then we will see face to face. Now I know only in part; then I will know fully, even as I have been fully known. and now faith, hope, and love abide, these three; and the greatest of these is love.

1 Corinthians 13:1–13, NRSV

The gift of the sun

The nineteenth-century preacher Robert Murray McCheyne died young but had made a significant impact in his seven years of ministry in Scotland. In this passage he makes reference to Jesus' telling his listeners in Matthew's Gospel that they should consider the 'lilies of the field, how they grow; they neither toil nor spin, yet ... even Solomon in all his glory was not clothed like one of these'.

It is all the gift of the sun, that the grass is of that refreshing green, and all the rivers are lines of waving blue. It is all the gift of the sun, that the flowers are tinged with their thousand glories; that the petal of the rose has its delicate blush, and the lily, which neither toils nor spins, has a brightness greater than Solomon's. Now this is the way you may be justified. You are dark and vile in yourselves, but Christ's glory shall be seen in you.

Robert Murray McCheyne (1813–1843)

Gloria in Excelsis

Gloria in Excelsis Deo (Latin for 'Glory to God in the highest') is the title and beginning of the Great Doxology used in the services of many Christian churches. It is derived from the longer and fuller version, used in the Byzantine Churches. The text of the song begins with a slight variation on the words sung by the angels as part of the announcement of the birth of Jesus to the shepherds in the field in Luke 2:14. The song continues with verses added to make a proper doxology. This song was originally in Greek and goes back to the early history of Christianity.

Glory be to God on high,
and in earth peace, good will towards men.

We praise thee, we bless thee,
we worship thee, we glorify thee,
we give thanks to thee for thy great glory.
O Lord God, heavenly King,
God the Father almighty.

O Lord, the only-begotten Son, Jesus Christ:
O Lord God, Lamb of God, Son of the Father,
that takest away the sins of the world,
have mercy upon us.
Thou that takest away the sins of the world,
receive our prayer.
Thou that sittest at the right hand of God the Father,
have mercy upon us.

For thou only art holy;
thou only art the Lord;
thou only, O Christ,
with the Holy Ghost,
art the Most High,
in the glory of God the Father.
Amen.

Common Worship, 2000

Glory to God the Trinity

Thomas Ken was born in Hertfordshire in 1637. He was a chaplain to King Charles II, appointed to be a bishop in the Church of England in 1684 and was one of the fathers of modern English hymn writing. Although Ken wrote a lot of poetry as well as hymns, he is not regarded as a great poet; however, he had a combination of spiritual insight and a feeling for poetic taste. As an English hymn-writer he has had few equals.

To God the Father, who first loved us
And made us accepted in the Beloved;
To God the Son, who loved us, and washed us
From our sins in his own blood;
To God the Holy Ghost, who sheds the love of God
Abroad in our hearts,
Be all love and all glory,
From time and for eternity.

Thomas Ken (1637–1711)

Go with the Lord

The following blessing is from a book of meditations and prayers written with busy people especially in mind, Still Waters, Deep Waters. *The author is an Australian pastor and writer.*

Go, and know that the Lord goes with you: let him lead you each day into the quiet place of your heart, and where he will speak with you; know that he loves you and watches over you – that he listens to you in gentle understanding, that he is with you always, wherever you are and however you may feel: and may the blessing of God – Father, Son and Holy Spirit – be yours for ever.

Rowland Croucher (b. 1937)

God be in my head

The Books of Hours were the prayer books used by lay people in medieval times. Commissioned by royal family members, the nobility and wealthy patrons, they became status symbols, the jewels in the collections of book collectors. This well-known prayer is taken from a Book of Hours that was a 1514 service book used in Clare College, Cambridge.

God be in my head
and in my understanding;
God be in my eyes
and in my looking;
God be in my mouth
and in my speaking;
God be in my heart
and in my thinking;
God be at my end
and at my departing.
>   *Book of Hours, 1514*

God cannot fail

Hannah Whitall Smith was the daughter of an American Quaker family but she moved to England in 1872. After coming to a new understanding of spiritual victory, she and her husband organized meetings in the hope that others would find this same victory over sin through entering 'the higher Christian life'.

Would you like to get rid of your burdens? Do you not long to hand over the management of your unmanageable self into the hands of One who is able to manage you? Are you not tired and weary, and does not the rest I speak of look sweet to you? ...

Your part is simply to rest. His part is to sustain you, and he cannot fail.

Hannah Whitall Smith (1832–1911)

God in all things

This Celtic prayer appeared in the nineteenth-century collection of prayers, hymns, charms, incantations, blessings, runes, poems and songs of Scotland made by Alexander Carmichael and known as the Carmina Gadelica.

God to enfold me,
God to surround me,
God in my speaking,
God in my thinking.

God in my sleeping,
God in my waking,
God in my watching,
God in my hoping.

God in my life,
God in my lips,
God in my soul,
God in my heart.

God in my sufficing,
God in my slumber,
God in mine ever-living soul,
God in mine eternity.

Traditional Celtic

God knows me

Jim Packer is a British-born theologian and prolific writer, who moved to Canada in 1979. He is best known for the book, Knowing God, *from which the following passage is taken.*

What matters supremely, therefore, is not, in the last analysis, the fact that I know God, but the larger fact that underlies it – the fact that he knows me ...

This is momentous knowledge. There is unspeakable comfort – the sort of comfort that energises, be it said, not enervates – in knowing that God is constantly taking knowledge of me in love, and watching over me for my good. There is tremendous relief in knowing that his love to me is utterly realistic, based at every point on prior knowledge of the worst about me, so that no discovery now can disillusion him about me, in the way I am so often disillusioned about myself, and quench his determination to bless me.

J I Packer (b. 1926)

The God of Christians

Blaise Pascal was a brilliant mathematician who devoted the last eight years of his short life to philosophy and theology. His most famous work, Pensées *(Thoughts), was published after his death, in 1670.*

The God of Christians is not a God who is simply the author of mathematical truths, or of the order of the elements; that is the view of heathen and Epicureans. He is not merely a God who exercises providence over the life and fortunes of men, to bestow on those who worship him a long and happy life ... The God of Christians is a God of love and of comfort, a God who fills the soul and heart of those whom he possesses, a God who makes them conscious of their inward wretchedness, and his infinite mercy, who unites himself to their inmost soul, who fills it with humility and joy, with confidence and love, who renders them incapable of any other end than himself.

Blaise Pascal (1623–1662)

God of consolation

In this letter, the apostle Paul has been through a testing time as he writes to the church at Corinth. He lets them know that just as he has found help and strength, so he wants to pass this on to them so that they are helped in any difficulties they may be facing.

Blessed be the God and Father of our Lord Jesus Christ, the Father of mercies and the God of all consolation, who consoles us in all our affliction, so that we may be able to console those who are in any affliction with the consolation with which we ourselves are consoled by God.

2 Corinthians 1:3–4, NRSV

God of truth, deliver us

Leslie Weatherhead was a minister in London for almost thirty years. He was among the first to suggest that insights from psychology could be useful in the Christian ministry of healing.

From the cowardice that shrinks from new truth,
From the laziness that is content with half-truths,
From the arrogance which thinks it knows all truth,
O God of Truth, deliver us. Amen.

Leslie Weatherhead (1893–1975)

God sees the heart

When the prophet Samuel is sent to the family of Jesse to anoint the future king, he asks the Lord about each of Jesse's strong handsome sons in turn. Only when they have all been rejected does Jesse call forward his youngest son, the shepherd boy who will become the future King David.

But the LORD said to Samuel, 'Do not look on his appearance or on the height of his stature, because I have rejected him; for the LORD does not see as mortals see; they look on the outward appearance, but the LORD looks on the heart.'

1 Samuel 16:7, NRSV

God speaks

Aiden Wilson Tozer was an American Protestant pastor best known as the author of many books. Among them at least two, The Pursuit of God *and* The Knowledge of the Holy, *are regarded as Christian classics. His books stress the possibility of and need for a deeper relationship with God.*

God did not write a book and send it by messenger to be read at a distance by unaided minds. He spoke a book and lives in his spoken words, constantly speaking his words and causing the power of them to persist across the years.

A W Tozer (1897–1963)

God speaks out of silence

Elijah was feeling defeated and alone after Jezebel, the wife of King Ahab, threatened to kill him, and he fled to the wilderness. He then travelled to Horeb, the place where the people of God had received the Ten Commandments and God's presence had been accompanied by thunder and lightning. But Elijah experiences the presence of God in a very different way – God spoke to him in a still small voice, the gentlest whisper of 'sheer silence'.

Then the word of the LORD came to him, saying, 'What are you doing here, Elijah?' He answered, 'I have been very zealous for the LORD, the God of hosts; for the Israelites have forsaken your covenant, thrown down your altars, and killed your prophets with the sword. I alone am left, and they are seeking my life, to take it away.'

He said, 'Go out and stand on the mountain before the LORD, for the LORD is about to pass by.' Now there was a great wind, so strong that it was splitting mountains and breaking rocks in pieces before the LORD, but the LORD was not in the wind; and after the wind an earthquake, but the LORD was not in the earthquake; and after the earthquake a fire, but the LORD was not in the fire; and after the fire a sound of sheer silence.

1 Kings 19:9–12, NRSV

God's armour

In the second half of the apostle Paul's letter to the church at Ephesus he writes to encourage the church to grow as a body of united individuals. He urges them to take up the full protection of God's power.

Therefore take up the whole armour of God, so that you may be able to withstand on that evil day, and having done everything, to stand firm. Stand therefore, and fasten the belt of truth around your waist, and put on the breastplate of righteousness. As shoes for your feet put on whatever will make you ready to proclaim the gospel of peace. With all of these, take the shield of faith, with which you will be able to quench all the flaming arrows of the evil one. Take the helmet of salvation, and the sword of the Spirit, which is the word of God. Pray in the Spirit at all times in every prayer and supplication. To that end keep alert and always persevere in supplication for all the saints.

Ephesians 6:13–18, NRSV

God's best gift

Abraham Lincoln was the sixteenth President of the United States of America. He began his political career in his early twenties and was the first American president to be assassinated. He was not a member of any particular church but did attend Christian services and this quote indicates that a Christian upbringing had influenced him.

I believe that the Bible is the best gift that God ever gave to man. All the good from the Saviour of the world is communicated to us through this book. I have been driven many times to my knees by the overwhelming conviction that I had nowhere else to go.

Abraham Lincoln (1809–1865)

God's church will never perish

Oscar Romero was archbishop of San Salvador in El Salvador, South America. He advocated a non-violent form of liberation theology and was assassinated while celebrating Mass. His death prompted an international outcry and calls for reform in El Salvador. He is one of the ten twentieth-century martyrs who are depicted in statues above the Great West Door of Westminster Abbey, London.

Martyrdom is a grace of God that I do not believe I deserve.
But if God accepts the sacrifice of my life,
Let my blood be a seed of freedom and the sign that hope will
    soon be reality.
Let my death, if it is accepted by God,
Be for my people's freedom and a witness of hope.

You may say, if they succeed in killing me,
That I pardon and bless those who do it.
Would, indeed, they might be convinced not to waste their time
A bishop will die, God's church, which is the people, will never
    perish.

Oscar Romero (1917–1980)

God's first Bible

Clement, a Greek philosopher, united the traditions of Greek philosophy with Christian doctrine. Origen was his pupil in Alexandria and went on to become a renowned theologian.

The world is the first Bible that God made for the instruction of man.

Clement of Alexandria (c. 150–c. 215)

God's glory revealed

*Andrew Murray was born in South Africa and became a well-known
missionary leader in the Dutch Reformed Church. He spoke widely and made
many evangelistic tours, but is best remembered for his writing. He produced
240 volumes of devotional writing and many are still widely read today.*

Telescopes have long discovered the wonders of God's
universe. By means of photography, new wonders of that glory
have been revealed. A photographic plate fixed below the
telescope will reveal millions of stars which otherwise could
never have been seen by the eye. Man must step to one side and
allow the glory of the heavens to reveal itself.

The stars, at first wholly invisible, will leave their image on
the plate.

Let your heart be as a photographic plate that waits for
God's glory to be revealed. The plate must be prepared and
clean; let your heart be prepared and purified by God's Spirit.
'God blesses those whose hearts are pure, for they will see God'
(Matthew 5:8). The plate must be immovable; let your heart be
still before God in prayer. The plate must be exposed for several
hours to receive the full impression of the farthest stars; let your
heart take time in silent waiting upon God and he will reveal his
glory.

If you keep silent before God and give him time, he will leave
within you impressions that will be as the rays of his glory
shining in you.

Andrew Murray (1828–1917)

God's grandeur

Gerard Manley Hopkins was an English poet and a Jesuit priest. He suffered from depression and died in Dublin relatively young, of typhoid fever. After his death he came to be regarded as one of the foremost Victorian poets. This is one of his most famous verses.

The world is charged with the grandeur of God.
It will flame out, like shining from shook foil;
It gathers to a greatness, like the ooze of oil
Crushed. Why do men then now not wreck his rod?
Generations have trod, have trod, have trod;
And all is seared with trade; bleared, smeared with toil;
And wears man's smudge and shares man's smell: the soil
is now bare, nor can foot feel, being shod.
And for all this, nature is never spent;
There lives the dearest freshness deep down things;
And though the last lights off the black West went
Oh, morning, at the brown brink eastward, springs –
Because the Holy Ghost over the bent
World broods with warm breast and with ah! bright wings.

Gerard Manley Hopkins (1844–1889)

God's means of deliverance

Watchman Nee was a Chinese Christian, author and church leader. He was imprisoned for his faith from 1952 until his death in 1972. His best-known work, based on the first part of the book of Romans, is The Normal Christian Life.

God's means of delivering us from sin is not by making us stronger and stronger, but by making us weaker and weaker. That is surely rather a peculiar way of victory, you say; but it is the divine way. God sets us free from the dominion of sin, not by strengthening our old man but by crucifying him; not by helping him to do anything, but by removing him from the scene of action.

Watchman Nee (1903–1972)

God's word

Martin Luther was a German monk and church reformer. The Bible was extremely important to him and his ideas were central to the Protestant Reformation. In this extract he affirms the importance of Scripture.

We must make a great difference between God's word and the word of man. A man's word is a little sound which flies into the air, and soon vanishes; but the word of God is greater than heaven and earth, yes, it is greater than death and hell, for it is the power of God, and remains everlastingly. Therefore we ought diligently to search God's word, and we must know certainly and believe that God himself speaks with us.

Martin Luther (1483–1546)

A good exchange

Jim Elliot was an evangelical Christian missionary who was killed in Ecuador along with four others while attempting to evangelize a violent Indian tribe then known as the Aucas. His journal entry for 28 October 1949 contains his now-famous quotation, expressing his belief that mission work was more important than life itself.

He is no fool who gives what he cannot keep to gain that which he cannot lose.

Jim Elliot (1927–1956)

The Good Samaritan

Jesus often taught in parables and the Gospel of Luke records one of the best-known of Jesus' stories. In reply to a question about who the neighbour is that you should love as you love yourself, Jesus tells the story of the Good Samaritan. He makes it clear that your neighbour is anyone in need.

Just then a lawyer stood up to test Jesus. 'Teacher,' he said, 'what must I do to inherit eternal life?' He said to him, 'What is written in the law? What do you read there?' He answered, 'You shall love the Lord your God with all your heart, and with all your soul, and with all your strength, and with all your mind; and your neighbour as yourself.' And he said to him, 'You have given the right answer; do this, and you will live.'

But wanting to justify himself, he asked Jesus, 'And who is my neighbour?' Jesus replied, 'A man was going down from Jerusalem to Jericho, and fell into the hands of robbers, who stripped him, beat him, and went away, leaving him half dead. Now by chance a priest was going down that road; and when he saw him, he passed by on the other side. So likewise a Levite, when he came to the place and saw him, passed by on the other side. But a Samaritan while travelling came near him; and when he saw him, he was moved with pity. He went to him and bandaged his wounds, having poured oil and wine on them. Then he put him on his own animal, brought him to an inn, and took care of him. The next day he took out two denarii, gave them to the innkeeper, and said, "Take care of him; and when I come back, I will repay you whatever more you spend." Which of these three, do you think, was a neighbour to the man who fell into the hands of the robbers?' He said, 'The one who showed him mercy.' Jesus said to him, 'Go and do likewise.'

Luke 10:25–37, NRSV

The grace

The grace is said at the close of many church services, as a blessing on all present. It is taken from the close of the apostle Paul's second letter to the Corinthian church (2 Corinthians 13:14).

The grace of our Lord Jesus Christ, and the love of God, and the fellowship of the Holy Ghost, be with us all evermore. Amen.

Book of Common Prayer (1928)

Guard me

The following anonymous Irish prayer seeks the help of Christ in resisting the everyday temptations that can lead us astray from truly living and working as faithful Christians.

Guard for me my eyes, Jesus Son of Mary, lest seeing
    another's wealth make me covetous.
Guard for me my ears, lest they hearken to slander, lest they
    listen constantly to folly in the sinful world.
Guard for me my heart, O Christ, in thy love, lest I ponder
    wretchedly the desire of any iniquity.
Guard for me my hands, that they be not stretched out for
    quarrelling, that they may not, after that, practice
    shameful supplication.
Guard for me my feet upon the gentle earth [of Ireland], lest,
    bent on profitless errands, they abandon rest.
Amen.

Anon.

Happy and peaceful

John Duns Scotus was a thirteenth-century Franciscan theologian and philosopher. He was known as 'Doctor Subtilis' because of his subtle merging of differing views. However, philosophers in the sixteenth century were not so complimentary about his work, and accused him of sophistry. This led to his name, 'dunce' (which developed from the name 'Dunse' given to his sixteenth-century followers), which became synonymous with 'someone incapable of scholarship'. This also led to the use of the 'dunce's cap' to punish pupils who behaved badly in class.

It is impossible that a nature should be perfectly happy and perfectly at peace unless it be wholly at peace and not only in part. Therefore the will cannot be at peace without the intellect, nor conversely, for each is a power of the one undivided nature. Consequently, beatitude consists in the perfection of both powers.

John Duns Scotus (c. 1266–1308)

Have mercy on me

Saint Anselm of Canterbury was an Italian medieval philosopher, theologian, and church official who was Archbishop of Canterbury between 1093 and 1109. He is famous as the archbishop who openly opposed the Crusades. In this prayer for mercy and forgiveness he also seeks the help of God in order to live a good life.

Almighty God, merciful Father, and my good Lord,
Have mercy on me, a sinner.
Grant me forgiveness of my sins.
Make me guard against and overcome
All snares, temptations and harmful pleasures.
May I shun utterly in word and in deed,
Whatever you forbid,
And do and keep whatever you command.
Let me believe and hope, love and live,
According to your purpose and your will.

St Anselm (1033–1109)

Help me to pray

German pastor Dietrich Bonhoeffer was a leader in the Confessing Church, which opposed the anti-Semitic policies of Adolf Hitler during the Second World War. He called for wider church resistance to Hitler's treatment of the Jews. In 1944 his connections to a group who had plotted to assassinate Hitler were uncovered and he was imprisoned. He was hanged just weeks before the liberation of Berlin by the Allies. This prayer is an indication of how his faith remained strong despite imprisonment.

O God, early in the morning I cry to you.
Help me to pray
And to concentrate my thoughts on you:
I cannot do this alone.
In me there is darkness,
But with you there is light;
I am lonely, but you do not leave me;
I am feeble in heart, but with you there is help;
I am restless, but with you there is peace.
In me there is bitterness, but with you there is patience;
I do not understand your ways,
But you know the way for me ...
Restore me to liberty,
And enable me to live now
That I may answer before you and before me.
Lord, whatever this day may bring,
Your name be praised.

Dietrich Bonhoeffer (1906–1945)

The help of God

Benedict founded the most famous monastery in Europe, on the heights of Monte Cassino, south of Rome. From there the Benedictine Order was founded and there he wrote his Rule, *which was based on the monastic understanding that salvation comes through disciplined godliness.*

First, I advise that you should implore the help of God to accomplish every good work you undertake; that he, who has now vouchsafed to rank us in the number of his children, may be no more grieved at our doing amiss. For we ought always to use his grace so faithfully in his service, as to give him no occasion to disinherit his children like an angry parent, or to punish for eternity his servants, like a master incensed at their crimes – servants who have refused to follow him in the way to glory.

Benedict of Nursia (480–547)

Holy desire

Written in the second half of the fourteenth century by an unknown author, believed to have been an English priest or a monk, The Cloud of Unknowing *is a spiritual guidebook that has influenced generations of seekers after spiritual truth.*

For it is not what you are or have been that God looks at with his merciful eyes, but what you would be. St Gregory asserts that 'all holy desires grow by delays; and if they fade because of these delays then they were never holy desires'. If a man feels less and less joy at new discoveries and the unexpected upsurge of his old and deliberate desires for good, then those desires never were holy. St Augustine is speaking of this holy desire when he says that 'the life of a good Christian consists of nothing else but holy desire'.

Farewell, spiritual friend, with God's blessing and mine upon you! And I pray Almighty God that true peace, sound counsel, and his own spiritual comfort and abundant grace may ever be with you and all his earthly lovers. Amen.

Anon. (14th century)

The Holy Spirit

*Gilbert Shaw was a barrister who became a priest and spiritual director.
Towards the end of his life he was involved in the development of the
contemplative life, for both women and men, and in particular with the
Sisters of the Love of God, at Fairacres, Oxford, to whom the following
homily was addressed.*

The Holy Spirit will never give you stuff on a plate – you've
got to work for it.

Your work is listening – taking the situation you're in and
holding it in courage, not being beaten down by it.

Your work is standing – holding things without being
deflected by your own desires or the desires of other people
round you. Then things work out just through patience. How
things alter we don't know, but the situation alters.

There must be dialogue in patience and charity – then
something seems to turn up that wasn't there before.

We must take people as they are and where they are – not
going too far ahead or too fast for them, but listening to their
needs and supporting them in their following.

The Holy Spirit brings things new and old out of the
treasure.

Intercessors bring the 'deaf and dumb' to Christ, that is their
part.

Seek for points of unity and stand on those rather than on
principles.

Have the patience that refuses to be pushed out; the patience
that refuses to be disillusioned.

There must be dialogue – or there will be no development.

Gilbert Shaw (1886–1967)

The hound of heaven

The religious poem 'The hound of heaven' runs to a total of 182 lines but its opening is well known. It became Francis Thompson's best-known work and was apparently admired by J R R Tolkein. Thompson describes God's relentless pursuit of human beings and the many and varied ways in which we try to avoid his divine grace.

I fled him, down the nights and down the days;
I fled him, down the arches of the years;
I fled him, down the labyrinthine ways
Of my own mind; and in the mist of tears
I hid from him, and under running laughter.
Up vistaed hopes I sped;
And shot, precipitated,
Adown Titanic glooms of chasmed fears,
From those strong Feet that followed, followed after.
But with unhurrying chase,
And unperturbèd pace,
Deliberate speed, majestic instancy,
They beat – and a Voice beat
More instant than the Feet –
'All things betray thee, who betrayest me.'

Halts by me that footfall:
Is my gloom, after all,
Shade of His hand, outstretched caressingly?
'Ah, fondest, blindest, weakest,
I am he whom thou seekest!
Thou dravest love from thee, who dravest me.'

Francis Thompson (1859–1907)

How children learn

This observation on children is often seen quoted on cards, samplers and elsewhere. Because it addresses the attitudes we display towards children and has nothing to do with what we are or not able to give them in material terms, it remains as true today as when it was written.

Children learn what they observe.

If children live with criticism, they learn to condemn and be judgmental.

If children live with hostility, they learn to be angry and fight.

If children live with ridicule, they learn to be shy and withdrawn.

If children live with shame, they learn to feel guilt.

If children live with tolerance, they learn to be patient.

If children live with encouragement they learn confidence.

If children live with praise, they learn to appreciate.

If children live with security, they learn to have faith.

If children live with approval, they learn to like themselves.

If children live with acceptance and friendship, they learn to find love in the world.

Dorothy Law Nolte (1924–2005)

How do I love thee?

Elizabeth Barrett Browning was a highly respected Victorian poet, the eldest of twelve children and an invalid from her teens. Her most famous work is Sonnets from the Portuguese, *a collection of love sonnets. By far the most famous poem from this collection, with one of the most famous opening lines in the English language, is number 43.*

How do I love thee? Let me count the ways.
I love thee to the depth and breadth and height
My soul can reach, when feeling out of sight
For the ends of being and ideal grace.
I love thee to the level of every day's
Most quiet need, by sun and candlelight.
I love thee freely, as men strive for right;
I love thee purely, as they turn from praise.
I love thee with a passion put to use
In my old griefs, and with my childhood faith.
I love thee with a love I seemed to lose
With my lost saints – I love thee with the breath,
Smiles, tears, of all my life!
And, if God choose,
I shall but love thee better after death.

Elizabeth Barrett Browning (1806–1861)

Humility

John Charles Ryle was the first Anglican bishop of Liverpool. He was a prolific writer, vigorous preacher, and faithful pastor. He was born at Macclesfield and educated at Eton and Christ Church, Oxford. He was a fine athlete who rowed and played cricket for Oxford, where he studied Classics. The son of a wealthy banker, he was destined for a career in politics before answering a call to ordained ministry.

If the only-begotten Son of God, the King of kings, did not think it beneath him to do the humblest work of a servant, there is nothing which his disciples should think themselves too great or too good to do.

J C Ryle (1816–1900)

Hymn to God the Father

Ben Jonson was born in London and became an actor, poet and playwright. William Shakespeare was among the cast in the first production of one of his plays. His best-known works are Volpone *and* The Alchemist *but he found great success as a writer of song lyrics.*

Hear me, O God!
A broken heart
Is my best part.
Use still thy rod,
That I may prove
Therein thy Love.

If thou hadst not
Been stern to me,
But left me free,
I had forgot
Myself and thee.

For sin's so sweet,
As minds ill-bent
Rarely repent,
Until they meet
Their punishment.

Who more can crave
Than thou hast done,
That gav'st a Son,
To free a slave?
First made of nought;
With all since bought.

Sin, Death, and Hell
His glorious Name
Quite overcame,
Yet I rebel
And slight the same.

But I'll come in
Before my loss
Me farther toss,
As sure to win
Under his cross.
Ben Jonson (1572–1637)

I arise today

*Saint Patrick was a Christian missionary and is a patron saint of Ireland.
This prayer is part of what is known as 'St Patrick's Breastplate' because of
those parts of it which seek God's protection. It is also sometimes called 'The
Deer's Cry' or 'The Lorica'.*

I arise today
Through God's strength to pilot me:
God's might to uphold me,
God's wisdom to guide me,
God's eye to look before me,
God's ear to hear me,
God's word to speak for me,
God's hand to guard me,
God's way to lie before me,
God's shield to protect me,
God's host to save me
From snares of devils,
From temptations of vices,
From everyone who shall wish me ill,
Afar and anear,
Alone and in multitude.

St Patrick (c. 389–c. 461)

I asked for peace

The following verses are by Digby Mackworth Dolben, a poet who drowned in an accident. His work was brought to public attention by Robert Bridges, a distant cousin, who edited the poems.

I asked for Peace:
My sins arose,
And bound me close,
I could not find release.

I asked for Truth:
My doubts came in,
And with their din
They wearied all my youth.

I asked for Love:
My lovers failed,
And griefs assailed
Around, beneath, above.

I asked for thee:
And thou didst come
To take me home
Within thy heart to be.
Digby Mackworth Dolben (1848–1867)

I believe

The Apostles' Creed is the baptismal creed used in the Western Church, and it is also recited at the daily offices of Morning and Evening Prayer. At one time it was believed that the Creed was composed by the twelve Apostles, each of whom contributed one clause.

I Believe in God the Father Almighty, Maker of heaven and earth: And in Jesus Christ his only Son our Lord, Who was conceived by the Holy Ghost, Born of the Virgin Mary, Suffered under Pontius Pilate, Was crucified, dead, and buried: He descended into hell; The third day he rose again from the dead; He ascended into heaven, And sitteth on the right hand of God the Father Almighty; From thence he shall come to judge the quick and the dead. I believe in the Holy Ghost; The holy Catholic Church; The Communion of Saints; The Forgiveness of sins; The Resurrection of the body, And the life everlasting. Amen.

Book of Common Prayer (1928)

I felt my heart strangely warmed

John Wesley was the fifteenth child of Samuel and Susanna Wesley. Samuel was a Church of England clergyman and the family lived at Epworth Rectory in Lincolnshire. At the age of five, John was rescued from the burning rectory. This escape made a deep impression on his mind and he regarded himself as providentially set apart, as a 'brand plucked from the burning'. John Wesley went on to become an Anglican minister and Christian theologian who was an early leader in the Methodist movement. This was the first widely successful evangelical movement in the United Kingdom.

I think it was about five this morning that I opened my Testament on those words: 'There are given unto us exceeding great and precious promises, even that ye should be partakers of the divine nature' (2 Peter 1:4). Just as I went out, I opened it again on those words: 'Thou art not far from the kingdom of God.' In the afternoon I was asked to go to St Paul's. The anthem was, 'Out of the deep have I called unto thee, O Lord: Lord, hear my voice. O let thine ears consider well the voice of my complaint. If thou, Lord, wilt be extreme to mark what is done amiss, O Lord, who may abide it? But there is mercy with thee; therefore thou shalt be feared. O Israel, trust in the Lord: for with the Lord there is mercy, and with him is plenteous redemption. And he shall redeem Israel from all his sins.'

In the evening I went very unwillingly to a society in Aldersgate Street, where one was reading Luther's preface to the Epistle to the Romans. About a quarter before nine, while he was describing the change which God works in the heart through faith in Christ, I felt my heart strangely warmed. I felt I did trust in Christ, Christ alone, for salvation; and an assurance was given me that he had taken away *my* sins, even *mine*, and saved *me* from the law of sin and death.

Wednesday, May 24th 1738

John Wesley (1703–1791)

I want to love

Michel Quoist, French parish priest and theologian, is best known for his devotional work Prayers of Life. *This prayer is a heart-felt expression of yearning.*

I want to love, Lord,
I need to love.
All my being is desire;
My heart,
My body,
Yearn in the night towards an unknown one to love.
My arms thrash about, and I can seize on no object for my love.
I am alone and want to be two.
I speak, and no one is there to listen.
I live, and no one is there to share my life.
Why be so rich and have no one to enrich?
Where does this love come from?
Where is it going?
I want to love, Lord,
I need to love.
Here, this evening, Lord, is all my love. ...

Michel Quoist (b. 1921)

*Voted the British public's favourite poem in 1995, Rudyard Kipling's 'If'
was published in 1910. Kipling was born in India and after attending
school in England returned to India at the age of sixteen and worked as a
journalist. It was here that he wrote many poems and stories. His most
famous work,* The Jungle Book, *was written later when he had married
and was living in America. He settled in England in 1896 and was
awarded the Nobel Prize for Literature in 1907.*

If you can keep your head when all about you
Are losing theirs and blaming it on you,
If you can trust yourself when all men doubt you,
But make allowance for their doubting too;
If you can wait and not be tired by waiting,
Or being lied about, don't deal in lies,
Or being hated, don't give way to hating,
And yet don't look too good, nor talk too wise:

If you can dream – and not make dreams your master;
If you can think – and not make thoughts your aim;
If you can meet with Triumph and Disaster
And treat those two impostors just the same;
If you can bear to hear the truth you've spoken
Twisted by knaves to make a trap for fools,
Or watch the things you gave your life to, broken,
And stoop and build 'em up with worn-out tools:

If you can make one heap of all your winnings
And risk it on one turn of pitch-and-toss,
And lose, and start again at your beginnings
And never breathe a word about your loss;
If you can force your heart and nerve and sinew
To serve your turn long after they are gone,
And so hold on when there is nothing in you
Except the Will which says to them: 'Hold on!'

If you can talk with crowds and keep your virtue,
Or walk with Kings – nor lose the common touch,
If neither foes nor loving friends can hurt you,
If all men count with you, but none too much;
If you can fill the unforgiving minute
With sixty seconds' worth of distance run,
Yours is the Earth and everything that's in it,
And – which is more – you'll be a Man, my son!

Rudyard Kipling (1865–1936)

Illumine our darkness

Daniil Savvich Tuptalo was born in 1651, not far from Kiev. He was born into a pious family and grew up a deeply believing Christian. In 1668 he became a monk and took the name Dimitrii. A writer and preacher, he had an ascetic lifestyle. Saint Dimitrii of Rostov remains an example of a saintly, non-covetous life for all Orthodox Christians. At his death, in October 1709, he was found with very few possessions, except for books and manuscripts. The following prayer is used at funerals or in times of trouble.

Come, our Light, and illumine our darkness.

Come, our Life, and raise us from death.

Come, our Physician, and heal our wounds.

Come, Flame of divine Love, and burn up the thorns of our sins, kindling our hearts with the flame of thy love.

Come, our King, sit upon the throne of our hearts and reign there.

For thou alone art our King and our Lord.

St Dimitrii of Rostov (1651–1709)

Imitating Christ

Thomas à Kempis was a Catholic monk and author of what is possibly the best-known book on Christian devotion, The Imitation of Christ.

'He that followeth me, walketh not in darkness,' saith the Lord. These are the words of Christ, by which we are taught to imitate his life and manners, if we would be truly enlightened, and be delivered from all blindness of heart. Let therefore our chief endeavour be to meditate upon the life of Jesus Christ.

Thomas à Kempis (c. 1380–1471)

Immortality

William Jennings Bryan was an American politician and lawyer, who was nominated three times for election as President of the United States. He served as US Secretary of State between 1913 and 1915 and was known as 'The Great Commoner' because of his total faith in the goodness and rightness of the common people.

Christ gave us proof of immortality, and yet it would hardly seem necessary that one should rise from the dead to convince us that the grave is not the end. To every created thing God has given a tongue that proclaims the resurrection.

If the Father deigns to touch with divine power the cold and pulseless heart of the buried acorn and to make it burst forth from its prison walls, will he leave neglected in the earth the soul of man, made in the image of his Creator?

William Jennings Bryan (1860–1925)

The importance of Christianity

Clive Staples Lewis was an Irish-born writer and scholar. An atheist from the age of fifteen he slowly returned to faith in his early thirties. He is perhaps best known for The Chronicles of Narnia *books. This insightful quotation shows us the true significance of Christianity.*

Christianity, if false, is of *no* importance, and, if true, is of infinite importance. The one thing it cannot be is moderately important.

C S Lewis (1898–1963)

Into the desert

The Desert Fathers chose, in the fourth century, to live the life of hermits in the desert in order to reclaim a faith that had become institutionalized after the conversion of Constantine and the adoption of Christianity by the Roman Empire.

One of the elders said: Just as a bee, wherever she goes, makes honey, so a monk, wherever he goes, if he goes to do the will of God, can always produce the spiritual sweetness of good works.

Thomas Merton (1915–1968)

An island prayer

The following prayer is believed to originate from the island group of Vanuatu, formerly known as the New Hebrides. These islands are part of the region north of Australia known as Melanesia. For island dwellers, many of whom will have depended on fishing, a safe boat would be their most important possession.

O Jesus,
Be the canoe that holds me in the sea of life.
Be the steer that keeps me straight.
Be the outrigger that supports me in times of great
    temptation.
Let thy spirit be my sail that carries me through each day.
Keep my body strong,
So that I can paddle steadfastly on,
In the long voyage of life.

Anon.

Jesus blesses children

The culture of his time held both children and women to be less important than men, but Jesus repeatedly defied convention, showing that in the eyes of God every human life was of equal value.

But when Jesus saw this, he was indignant and said to them, 'Let the little children come to me; do not stop them; for it is to such as these that the kingdom of God belongs. Truly I tell you, whoever does not receive the kingdom of God as a little child will never enter it.' And he took them up in his arms, laid his hands on them, and blessed them.

Mark 10:14–16, NRSV

Jesus Christ the apple tree

'Jesus Christ the Apple Tree' is a mystical poem, by an unknown New England author, found in the collection Divine Hymns or Spiritual Songs *by Joshua Smith of New Hampshire, dated 1784. Set to music it is well known and much loved as a Christmas carol.*

The tree of life my soul hath seen,
Laden with fruit and always green:
The trees of nature fruitless be
Compared with Christ the apple tree.

His beauty doth all things excel:
By faith I know, but ne'er can tell
The glory which I now can see
In Jesus Christ the apple tree.

For happiness I long have sought,
And pleasure dearly I have bought:
I missed of all; but now I see
'Tis found in Christ the apple tree.

I'm weary with my former toil,
Here I will sit and rest awhile:
Under the shadow I will be,
Of Jesus Christ the apple tree.

This fruit doth make my soul to thrive,
It keeps my dying faith alive;
Which makes my soul in haste to be
With Jesus Christ the apple tree.

Divine Hymns or Spiritual Songs (1784)

Jesus' hands

Margaret Cropper was born in Westmorland in the Lake District. She was a Quaker, and the family trait of serving the community guided her all of her life. During the First World War she worked to improve conditions for the girls in the munitions factories. Her children's hymn 'Jesus' Hands Were Kind Hands' has become a favourite, especially in North America.

Jesus' hands were kind hands,
Doing good to all;
Healing pain and sickness,
Blessing children small;
Washing tired feet
And saving those who fall;
Jesus' hands were kind hands,
Doing good to all.

Take my hands, Lord Jesus,
Let them work for you,
Make them strong and gentle,
Kind in all I do;
Let me watch you, Jesus,
Till I'm gentle too,
Till my hands are kind hands,
Quick to work for you.

Margaret Cropper (1886–1980)

Journey into God

Bonaventure was born John of Fidanza and given his new name on entering the Franciscan Order. He was appointed the leader of the Order in 1257. He is remembered as a spiritual writer and theologian and his best-known work is Journey of the Soul into God.

Whoever wishes to ascend to God must first avoid sin, which deforms our nature, then exercise his natural powers mentioned above: by praying, to receive restoring grace; by a good life, to receive purifying justice; by meditating, to receive illuminating knowledge; and by contemplating, to receive perfecting wisdom. Just as no one comes to wisdom except through grace, justice and knowledge, so no one comes to contemplation except by penetrating meditation, a holy life and devout prayer.

Bonaventure (1221–1274)

Journeying in faith

Christina Rossetti was born in London, one of four children of Italian parents. Her Christmas poem 'In the Bleak Midwinter' became widely known after her death when it was set as a Christmas carol. This poem, 'Uphill', was written in 1861.

Does the road wind uphill all the way?
Yes, to the very end.
Will the day's journey take the whole long day?
From morn to night, my friend.

But is there for the night a resting-place?
A roof for when the slow dark hours begin.
May not the darkness hide it from my face?
You cannot miss that inn.

Shall I meet other wayfarers at night?
Those who have gone before.
Then must I knock, or call when just in sight?
They will not keep you standing at that door.

Shall I find comfort, travel-sore and weak?
Of labour you shall find the sum.
Will there be beds for me and all who seek?
Yes, beds for all who come.

Christina Rossetti (1830–1894)

Joy to the world

This Christmas hymn was written by Isaac Watts when he was just fifteen years old. It is based on Psalm 98, which calls on the world to celebrate the King whom God has sent.

Joy to the world, the Lord is come!
Let earth receive her King;
Let every heart prepare him room,
And heaven and nature sing,
And heaven and nature sing,
And heaven, and heaven, and nature sing.

Joy to the earth, the Saviour reigns!
Let men their songs employ;
While fields and floods, rocks, hills and plains
Repeat the sounding joy,
Repeat the sounding joy,
Repeat, repeat, the sounding joy.

No more let sins and sorrows grow,
Nor thorns infest the ground;
He comes to make his blessings flow
Far as the curse is found,
Far as the curse is found,
Far as, far as, the curse is found.

He rules the world with truth and grace,
And makes the nations prove
The glories of his righteousness,
And wonders of his love,
And wonders of his love,
And wonders, wonders, of his love.

Isaac Watts (1647–1748)

Justification of believers

John Davenant was a professor of Divinity at Cambridge and also Bishop of Salisbury for the last twenty years of his life. His most enduring piece of writing is his Exposition of Colossians.

The justification of believers does not rest on this, that they have in themselves a quality of new righteousness, which they would venture to subject to a legal examination of the strict judgment of God; but that, by and through the merits of the Redeemer, in whom they believe, they are not to undergo such judgments, but are dealt with as if they had in themselves exact legal righteousness.

John Davenant (1576–1641)

Keep us, Lord

John Donne was a Jacobean poet and preacher, whose many works include sonnets, love poetry and religious poems. Having married the love of his life in defiance of her father he lived in poverty for years. After her death at the age of thirty-three he was heartbroken. This prayer speaks of both the privileges and also the duties of being a Christian.

Keep us, Lord, so awake in the duties of our calling that we may sleep in thy peace and wake in thy glory.

John Donne (1572–1631)

Keep us through winter

Samuel Longfellow, brother of the poet Henry Longfellow, was an American clergyman and hymn-writer. He was known for his focus on children, his kind and optimistic disposition, and his poetical expression of Christianity. In this poem, 'Winter now', he reminds us that the warmth of God's love endures through the coldest and bleakest weather.

'Tis winter now; the fallen snow
Has left the heavens all coldly clear;
Through leafless boughs the sharp winds blow,
And all the earth lies dead and drear.

And yet God's love is not withdrawn;
His life within the keen air breathes;
His beauty paints the crimson dawn,
And clothes the boughs with glittering wreaths.

And though abroad the sharp winds blow,
And skies are chill, and frosts are keen,
Home closer draws her circle now,
And warmer glows her light within.

O God! Who giv'st the winter's cold
As well as summer's joyous rays,
Us warmly in thy love enfold,
And keep us through life's wintry days.

Samuel Longfellow (1819–1892)

The Lamb

William Blake was a painter, poet and printmaker, whose work is much better known now than it was in his lifetime. 'The Lamb' was part of Blake's Songs of Innocence *collection. It talks about God's love shown in his care for the lamb and the child and about the apparent paradox, that God became both child and Lamb in coming, as Jesus, into the world.*

Little Lamb, who made thee?
Dost thou know who made thee?
Gave thee life, and bid thee feed,
By the stream and o'er the mead;
Gave thee clothing of delight,
Softest clothing, woolly, bright;
Gave thee such a tender voice,
Making all the vales rejoice?
Little Lamb, who made thee?
Dost thou know who made thee?

Little Lamb, I'll tell thee,
Little Lamb, I'll tell thee.
He is called by thy name,
For he calls himself a Lamb.
He is meek, and he is mild;
He became a little child.
I a child, and thou a lamb,
We are called by his name.
Little Lamb, God bless thee!
Little Lamb, God bless thee!

William Blake (1757–1827)

Last lines

Anne Brontë wrote this poem a few weeks after the death of her sister Emily. She knew that she too had contracted tuberculosis and would probably not live long.

I hoped, that with the brave and strong,
My portioned task might lie;
To toil amid the busy throng,
With purpose pure and high.

But God has fixed another part,
And He has fixed it well;
I said so with my bleeding heart,
When first the anguish fell.

A dreadful darkness closes in
On my bewildered mind;
Oh, let me suffer and not sin,
Be tortured, yet resigned.

Shall I with joy thy blessings share
And not endure their loss?
Or hope the martyr's crown to wear
And cast away the cross?

Thou, God, hast taken our delight,
Our treasured hope away;
Thou bidst us now weep through the night
And sorrow through the day.

These weary hours will not be lost,
These days of misery,
These nights of darkness, anguish-tost,
Can I but turn to thee.

Weak and weary though I lie,
Crushed with sorrow, worn with pain,
I may lift to heaven mine eye,
And strive to labour not in vain;

That inward strife against the sins
That ever wait on suffering
To strike whatever first begins –
Each ill that would corruption bring;

That secret labour to sustain
With humble patience every blow;
To gather fortitude from pain,
And hope and holiness from woe.

Thus let me serve thee from my heart,
Whate'er may be my written fate:
Whether thus early to depart,
Or yet a while to wait.

If thou shouldst bring me back to life,
More humbled I should be;
More wise, more strengthened for the strife,
More apt to lean on thee.

Should death be standing at the gate,
Thus should I keep my vow;
But, Lord! whatever be my fate,
Oh, let me serve thee now!

Anne Brontë (1820–1849)

Latimer's last words

Hugh Latimer took part, with Thomas Cranmer and Nicholas Ridley, in the Oxford disputations against a group of Catholic theologians and would not recant his Protestant faith. On 16 October 1555, Ridley and Latimer were led to their martyrdom. Ridley was fully robed, dressed as a bishop. Latimer wore a simple frieze frock. The seventy-year-old Latimer followed feebly behind Ridley. Ridley gave his clothes away to those standing by and Latimer quietly stripped to his shroud. As they were fastened to their stakes, Ridley's brother tied a bag of gunpowder to each of their necks. And then, as a burning faggot was laid at the feet of Ridley, Latimer spoke his famous words.

Be of good comfort, Master Ridley, and play the man; we shall this day light such a candle, by God's grace, in England, as I trust shall never be put out.

Hugh Latimer (c. 1485–1555)

Let nothing disturb thee

Teresa Avila was born in Avila, Spain. In 1534, at the age of twenty, she entered the monastery of the Incarnation of the Carmelite nuns at Avila, where she often suffered from illness. In 1559, Teresa became firmly convinced that Christ was present to her in bodily form, though invisible. This vision lasted almost uninterruptedly for more than two years. She died in 1582, having founded a number of convents, and was canonized forty years after her death.

Let nothing disturb thee, nothing afright thee;
All things are passing;
God never changeth;
Patient endurance attaineth to all things;
Who God possesseth in nothing is wanting;
Alone God sufficeth.

Teresa of Avila (1515–1582)

Let us make a joyful noise

This call to worship from Psalm 95 has been used as the basis for a number of popular hymns and worship songs. It acknowledges God as the creator of all things and as deserving of our praise.

O come, let us sing to the LORD;
let us make a joyful noise to the rock of our salvation!
Let us come into his presence with thanksgiving;
let us make a joyful noise to him with songs of praise!
For the LORD is a great God,
and a great King above all gods.
In his hand are the depths of the earth;
the heights of the mountains are his also.
The sea is his, for he made it,
and the dry land, which his hands have formed.

O come, let us worship and bow down,
let us kneel before the LORD, our Maker!
For he is our God,
and we are the people of his pasture,
and the sheep of his hand.

Psalm 95:1–7, NRSV

Life be in my speech

The following is part of a hymn that was sung before a pilgrim set out on his journey. A pilgrimage might be dangerous and the traveller might not return, but he prays for a journey in which he might show love to and receive love from those he encounters on the way.

Life be in my speech,
Sense in what I say,
The bloom of cherries on my lips,
Till I come back again.

The love Christ Jesus gave
Be filling every heart for me,
The love Christ Jesus gave
Filling me for every one.

Anon.

Life is a hard fight

Florence Nightingale was a pioneer of modern nursing and a writer. She was a Christian who felt sure that God had called her to be a nurse. This choice of career was most unusual for a woman born into an upper-class family, at a time when nurses were more usually camp followers during wartime who both cooked for the soldiers and tended to the wounded. In the Crimea in the 1850s Florence realized that many of the deaths in the barracks hospital were due to the insanitary conditions. Ten times more soldiers died from illnesses such as typhus, typhoid, cholera and dysentery than from battle wounds.

Life is a hard fight, a struggle, a wrestling with the principle of evil, hand to hand, foot to foot. Every inch of the way is disputed. The night is given to us to take breath and to pray, to drink deep at the fountain of power. The day, to use the strength which has been given to us, to go forth to work with it till the evening.

Florence Nightingale (1820–1910)

Like a reservoir

Bernard of Clairvaux was a French abbot and a founder of the Cistercian Order, which had begun as a community of reformed Benedictines at Cîteaux. When this community grew too large it planted new communities and Clairvaux was founded in 1115 with Bernard appointed as its abbot. Bernard became extremely important within the church after he championed the successful claimant to the papacy following the disputed election in 1130. One result of Bernard's fame was the growth of the Cistercian order. Between 1130 and 1145, more than 90 monasteries in connection with Clairvaux were either founded or affiliated from other rules, three being established in England and one in Ireland.

If you are wise you will show yourself rather as a reservoir than a canal. For a canal spreads abroad the water it receives, but a reservoir waits until it is filled before overflowing, and thus shares without loss to itself its superabundance of water.

Bernard of Clairvaux (1091–1153)

Listening to that other voice

Clive Staples Lewis was an Irish-born writer and scholar. An atheist from the age of fifteen he slowly returned to faith in his early thirties and became a well-known Christian apologist. This quotation reminds us of the need to take control of life's events and to listen to the voice of the God who wants to change us.

The real problem of the Christian life comes where people do not usually look for it. It comes the very moment you wake up each morning. All your wishes and hopes for the day rush at you like wild animals. And the first job each morning consists simply in shoving them all back, in listening to that other voice, taking that other point of view, letting that other larger, stronger, quieter life come flowing in. And so on, all day. Standing back from all your natural fussings and frettings; coming in out of the wind.

We can only do it for moments at first. But from those moments the new sort of life will be spreading through our system: because now we are letting Him work at the right part of us. It is the difference between paint which is merely laid on the surface, and a dye or stain which soaks right through. He never talked vague, idealistic gas. When He said, 'Be perfect', He meant it. He meant that we must go in for the full treatment. It is hard; but the sort of compromise we are all hankering after is harder – in fact, it is impossible. It may be hard for an egg to turn into a bird: it would be a jolly sight harder for it to learn to fly while remaining an egg. We are like eggs at present. And you cannot go on indefinitely being just an ordinary decent egg. We must be hatched or go bad.

C S Lewis (1898–1963)

Live on the Lord Jesus

Charles Haddon Spurgeon was an English Baptist preacher who became a pastor at the age of just seventeen. He also founded the charity organization now known as Spurgeon's, which works worldwide with families and children. His sermons were translated into many languages in his lifetime and are still read and quoted from today by Christians of all denominations.

We never live so well as when we live on the Lord Jesus simply as he is, and not upon our enjoyments and raptures. Faith is never more likely to increase in strength than in times which seem adverse to her. When she is lightened of trust in joys, experiences, frames, feelings, and the like, she rises the nearer heaven. Trust in your Redeemer's strength, benighted soul; exercise what faith you have, and by and by he shall rise upon you with healing beneath his wings. Go from faith to faith and you shall receive blessing upon blessing.

Charles Haddon Spurgeon (1834–1892)

Look to your own faults

Jesus' teaching contains a number of warnings against hypocrisy and in this passage from Matthew's Gospel he warns his listeners against being concerned about other people's faults while overlooking their own.

'Do not judge, so that you may not be judged. For with the judgement you make you will be judged, and the measure you give will be the measure you get. Why do you see the speck in your neighbour's eye, but do not notice the log in your own eye? Or how can you say to your neighbour, "Let me take the speck out of your eye", while the log is in your own eye? You hypocrite, first take the log out of your own eye, and then you will see clearly to take the speck out of your neighbour's eye.'

Matthew 7:1–5, NRSV

Looking through the Bible

Phillips Brooks was an American clergyman and author who opposed slavery and was, for a short time, bishop of Massachusetts. He died just fifteen months after he was consecrated.

The Bible is like a telescope. If a man looks through his telescope, then he sees worlds beyond; but if he looks at his telescope, then he does not see anything but that. The Bible is a thing to be looked through, to see that which is beyond.

Phillips Brooks (1835–1893)

The Lord goes with you

This blessing has appeared in a number of prayer collections but its author is unknown. It was probably written in the twentieth century.

Go, and know that the Lord goes with you: let him lead you each day into the quiet place of your heart, where he will speak with you; know that he loves you and watches over you – that he listens to you in gentle understanding, that he is with you always, wherever you are and however you may feel: and may the blessing of God – Father, Son, and Holy Spirit – be yours for ever.

Anon.

The Lord is my shepherd

A number of the Psalms are attributed to the shepherd boy David, who become king after the death of Saul. It draws on images from his experience looking after his father's sheep and is perhaps the best-known Psalm of all.

The LORD is my shepherd, I shall not want.
He makes me lie down in green pastures;
he leads me beside still waters;
he restores my soul.
He leads me in right paths
for his name's sake.

Even though I walk through the darkest valley,
I fear no evil;
for you are with me;
your rod and your staff –
they comfort me.

You prepare a table before me
in the presence of my enemies;
you anoint my head with oil;
my cup overflows.
Surely goodness and mercy shall follow me
all the days of my life,
and I shall dwell in the house of the LORD
my whole life long.

Psalm 23, NRSV

Lord of the winds

Mary Coleridge, a great-grandniece of Samuel Taylor Coleridge, was an English novelist and poet, whose work was influenced by Christina Rossetti. A number of her poems have been set to music.

Lord of the winds, I cry to thee,
I that am dust,
And blown about by every gust
I fly to thee.

Lord of the waters, unto thee I call.
I that am weed upon the waters borne,
And by the waters torn,
Tossed by the waters, at thy feet I fall.

Mary Coleridge (1861–1907)

Lord, seek us

Christina Rossetti was a poet and sister of the artist Dante Gabriel Rossetti. She is known for her Christmas poem 'In the Bleak Midwinter'. In this poem, which has also been set to music, she seeks God's protection from earthly concerns.

O Lord, seek us, O Lord, find us
In thy patient care;
By thy love before, behind us,
Round us everywhere;
Lest the god of this world blind us,
Lest he speak us fair,
Lest he forge a chain to bind us,
Lest he bait a snare.
Turn not from us, call to mind us,
Find, embrace us, bear;
Be thy love before, behind us,
Round us, everywhere.

Christina Rossetti (1830–1894)

Lord, you never sleep

Psalm 121 is known as a 'Song of Ascents', probably written to be sung by the people of Israel as they journeyed to the temple for the celebration of a festival.

I lift up my eyes to the hills –
from where will my help come?
My help comes from the LORD,
who made heaven and earth.

He will not let your foot be moved;
he who keeps you will not slumber.
He who keeps Israel
will neither slumber nor sleep.

The LORD is your keeper;
the LORD is your shade at your right hand.
The sun shall not strike you by day,
nor the moon by night.

The LORD will keep you from all evil;
he will keep your life.
The LORD will keep
your going out and your coming in
from this time on and for evermore.

Psalm 121, NRSV

The Lord's meaning

Julian of Norwich was one of the great English mystics. Little is known about her life except her writings. Having narrowly survived death from illness at the age of 30 she fell seriously ill once more in 1373 and experienced a series of 16 revelatory visions, mostly concerning the passion of Christ. After her recovery she meditated on these visions and went on to record her thoughts. This extract records her meditation on love as the Lord's purpose in revealing himself to her.

And from the time that it was shown, I desired often to know what our Lord's meaning was. And fifteen years and more afterward I was answered in my spiritual understanding, thus: 'Would you know your Lord's meaning in this thing? Know it well, love was his meaning. Who showed it to you? Love. What did he show you? Love. Why did he show it? For love. Keep yourself therein and you shall know and understand more in the same. But you shall never know nor understand any other thing, forever.' Thus I was taught that love was our Lord's meaning. And I saw quite clearly in this and in all, that before God made us, he loved us, which love was never slaked nor ever shall be. And in this love he has done all his work, and in this love he has made all things profitable to us. And in this love our life is everlasting. In our creation we had a beginning. But the love wherein he made us was in him with no beginning. And all this shall be seen in God without end.

Julian of Norwich (c. 1342–c. 1416)

The Lord's Prayer

The Lord's Prayer is based on the words that Jesus taught his disciples, as reported in Matthew 6:9–13 and Luke 11:2–4. Although there are more modern versions in use today, the traditional rendering from the Book of Common Prayer remains very popular.

Our Father, who art in heaven,
Hallowed be thy Name.
Thy kingdom come.
Thy will be done,
On earth as it is in heaven.
Give us this day our daily bread.
And forgive us our trespasses,
As we forgive those who trespass against us.
And lead us not into temptation;
But deliver us from evil.
For thine is the kingdom, and the power, and the glory,
For ever and ever.
Amen.

Book of Common Prayer (1928)

The Lord's promise to Solomon

After twenty years of building work, Solomon had completed the temple for the Lord and the king's house and he dedicated the temple with sacrifices and prayer. The Lord appeared to Solomon and makes a promise.

If my people who are called by my name humble themselves, pray, seek my face, and turn from their wicked ways, then I will hear from heaven, and will forgive their sin and heal their land.

2 Chronicles 7:14, NRSV

Love, and go on

The following anonymous poem was used in Westminster Abbey at the start of the funeral of Queen Elizabeth, the Queen Mother, on 9 April 2002.

You can shed tears that she is gone
or you can smile because she has lived.
You can close your eyes and pray that she'll come back
or you can open your eyes and see all she's left.
Your heart can be empty because you can't see her
or you can be full of the love you shared.
You can turn your back on tomorrow and live yesterday
or you can be happy for tomorrow because of yesterday.
You can remember her and only that she's gone
or you can cherish her memory and let it live on.
You can cry and close your mind, be empty and turn your
    back
or you can do what she'd want: smile, open your eyes, love
and go on.

Anon.

Love bade me welcome

George Herbert, remembered as a writer of religious poems, was educated for the priesthood but his skills in oratory brought him to the attention of the court and instead he became a member of parliament. In his late thirties, however, he was ordained and he spent the rest of his life as a priest near Salisbury in Wiltshire.

Love bade me welcome: yet my soul drew back,
    Guilty of dust and sin.
But quick-ey'd Love, observing me grow slack
    From my first entrance in,
Drew nearer to me, sweetly questioning,
    If I lack'd any thing.

A guest, I answer'd, worthy to be here:
    Love said, You shall be he.
I the unkind, ungrateful? Ah, my dear,
    I cannot look on thee.
Love took my hand, and smiling did reply,
    Who made the eyes but I?

Truth Lord, but I have marr'd them: let my shame
    Go where it doth deserve.
And know you not, says Love, who bore the blame?
    My dear, then I will serve.
You must sit down, says Love, and taste my meat:
    So I did sit and eat.

George Herbert (1593–1633)

Love begins at home

Mother Teresa was born in Albania and became a Roman Catholic nun. She founded the Missionaries of Charity in Calcutta in 1950. For over forty years she ministered to the poor and to outcasts, while overseeing the expansion of the work of the Missionaries of Charity, first throughout India and then in other countries. In 1979 she was awarded the Nobel Peace Prize.

The following is an extract from an address she delivered in Cambridge on being awarded an honorary doctorate of the university.

Do we know our poor here and now? There may be poor within our own family: let us not forget that love begins at home. Do we know them? Do we know those who live alone? The unwanted? The forgotten?

One day I found among the debris a woman who was burning with fever. About to die, she kept repeating, 'It is my son who has done it!'

I took her in my arms and carried her home to the convent. On the way I urged her to forgive her son. It took a good while before I could hear her say, 'Yes, I forgive him.' She said it with a feeling of genuine forgiveness, just as she was about to pass away.

The woman was not aware that she was dying, that she was burning with fever, that she was suffering. What was breaking her heart was her own son's lack of love.

Saint John says, 'How can you say that you love God, whom you do not see, if you do not love your neighbour, whom you see?' He uses a strong expression for such an attitude: 'You are a liar if you say that you love God but do not love your neighbour' (see 1 John 4:20).

I think this is something we all have to understand: that love begins at home. In our day we see with growing clarity that the sorrows of the world have their origin in the family. We do not have time to look at each other, to exchange a greeting, to share a moment of joy. We take still less time to be what our children expect of us, what our spouse expects of us. And thus, each day we belong less and less to our own homes, and our contacts are less.

Where are our elderly people today? Usually in institutions. Where is the unborn child? Dead! Why? Because we do not want him.

I see a great poverty in the fact that in the West a child may have to die because we fear to feed one more mouth, we fear to educate one more child. The fear of having to feed an elderly person in the family means that this person is sent away.

One day, however, we will have to meet the Lord of the universe. What will we tell him about that child, about that old father or mother? They are his creatures, children of God. What will be our answer?

God has invested all his love in creating that human life. That is why we are not entitled to destroy it, especially we who know that Christ has died for the salvation of that life. Christ has died and has given everything for that child.

If we are really Christian, then for us too, as for that Hindu gentleman, 'Christianity is giving.' We have to give until it hurts. Love, in order to be genuine, has to have a cost. For Jesus the cost was loving us. Even God had a cost in loving: he gave us his Son.

There's nothing I can give you today because I have nothing. But what I desire from you is that when we look together and discover the poor in our families, we may begin to give love in our homes until it hurts. May we have a prompt smile. May we have time to devote to our people.

A few days ago, a man came toward me on the street and asked, 'Are you Mother Teresa?'

'Yes,' I answered.

He asked, 'Send one of your sisters to our home. I am half blind, and my wife is on the fringe of insanity. We long to hear the echo of a human voice. This is the only thing we miss.'

When I sent the sisters, they realised it was true. The couple lacked nothing materially. But they were being suffocated by the anguish of not having any relatives nearby. They felt unwanted, useless, unprofitable – doomed to die in utter loneliness.

This wounds Christ's heart. He loved to the point of suffering. But how will we be able to love the poor if we do not begin by loving the members of our own family?

Love – I will never get tired of saying it – *begins at home*.

Mother Teresa (1910–1997)

Love is as hard as nails

Clive Staples Lewis was an Irish-born writer and scholar. An atheist from the age of fifteen he slowly returned to his Christian faith in his early thirties. He wrote a number of books, and also poetry. The following poem considers the ways in which we think of love but also the harsh reality of the sacrificial love of Christ as seen on the cross.

Love's as warm as tears,
Love is tears:
Pressure within the brain,
Tension at the throat,
Deluge, weeks of rain,
Haystacks afloat,
Featureless seas between
Hedges, where once was green.

Love's as fierce as fire,
Love is fire:
All sorts – infernal heat
Clinkered with greed and pride,
Lyric desire, sharp-sweet,
Laughing, even when denied,
And that empyreal flame
Whence all loves came.

Love's as fresh as spring,
Love is spring:
Bird-song hung in the air,
Cool smells in a wood,
Whispering 'Dare! Dare!'
To sap, to blood,
Telling 'Ease, safety, rest,
Are good; not best.'

Love's as hard as nails,
Love is nails:
Blunt, thick, hammered through
The medial nerves of One
Who, having made us, knew
The thing he had done,
Seeing (with all that is)
Our cross, and his.

C S Lewis (1898–1963)

Love's self-opening

John Taylor was Bishop of Winchester and had worked in Africa for the Church Missionary Society. He is best known for his book The Go-Between God, *an exploration of the doctrine of the Holy Spirit. The following poem was inspired by Rublev's icon of the Holy Trinity.*

Love in its fullness loomed, love
Loomed at the tent door in its truth,
Not the sole unique truth
Reserved for the incomparable God,
But for a love consisting of communion.
I, Abraham, looked for a single
Flower; but it has blossomed into a
Multiple head, made for sharing.
Love's ultimate reality, gazing at the Son
Proclaims 'I AM'.
And he, as love's delight,
Says 'look and see'.
Their mutuality precedes creation
Being Eternal, and offers the only space
In which it can exist.
So the cup of suffering at which they gaze
Is the price already paid
For the world's pardon. 'The Lamb
Slain before the foundation
Of the world.'

John Vernon Taylor (1914–2001)

Loving Communion

The following anonymous poem brings out both the significance of the bread and the wine of Communion and also the importance of not sharing in this sacrament without proper thought and attention. This reading, the first part of which is believed to be Celtic in origin, is sometimes used, with responses, to introduce Communion.

Be gentle, when you touch bread,
Let it not be uncared for, unwanted.
So often bread is taken for granted.
There is so much beauty in bread,
Beauty of sun and soil,
Beauty of patient toil.
Winds and rain have caressed it,
Christ often blessed it;
Be gentle when you touch bread.

Be loving when you drink wine,
So freely received and joyfully shared
In the spirit of him who cared;
Warm as a flowing river,
Shining as clear as the sun,
Deep as the soil
Of human toil,
The winds and air caressed it,
Christ often blessed it,
Be loving when you drink wine.

Anon.

Loving God above all things

Susanna Wesley was herself the youngest of twenty-four children and after marrying Samuel Wesley she had nineteen children of her own. Only eight of them survived beyond her death, but two of these, John and Charles, went on to lead the movement that became the Methodist Church. Susanna was almost solely responsible for the education of her children and she also wrote commentaries and prayers.

God, I give you the praise for days well spent.
But I am yet unsatisfied,
Because I do not enjoy enough of you.
I apprehend myself at too great a distance from you.
I would have my soul more closely united to you by faith and
    love.
You know, Lord, that I would love you above all things.
You know me, you know my desires, my expectations.
My joys all centre in you and it is you that I desire.
It is your favour, your acceptance, the communications of
    your grace that I earnestly wish for more than anything in
    the world.

Susanna Wesley (1669–1742)

Loving God in all things

This prayer, or collect, has been in the prayer book of the Church of England, almost unchanged, since the 1662 Book of Common Prayer.

O God, who hast prepared for them that love thee
such good things as pass our understanding:
pour into our hearts such love toward thee
that we, loving thee in all things and above all things,
may obtain thy promises
which exceed all that we can desire;
through Jesus Christ thy Son our Lord,
who liveth and reigneth with thee,
in the unity of the Holy Spirit,
one God, now and for ever.
Amen.

Common Worship, 2000

Made for good works

In this letter to the church in Ephesus, Paul explains that faith in Christ and a realization of how much God loves us should be a spur to godly action. We are not saved by works, but faith is often shown by what we do and say.

For we are what he has made us, created in Christ Jesus for good works, which God prepared beforehand to be our way of life.

Ephesians 2:10, NRSV

Magnify God's glory

Andrew Murray was born in South Africa and became a well-known
missionary leader in the Dutch Reformed Church. He spoke widely and made
many evangelistic tours, but is best remembered for his writing. He produced
240 volumes of devotional writing and many are still widely read today.

God's glory, you understand, is seen primarily in his
goodness, and so for us to give glory to God means that we
magnify his goodness. Now, to magnify something, you make it
look larger, increasing it out of proportion. To talk about
ourselves or our activities out of true proportion is dangerous
indeed, but when we magnify God, we are on safe ground. We
simply cannot say too much about God's goodness and love. The
most exaggerated things we can think of will still be far below
what is actually the case. So we can freely and joyfully join with
the Psalmist who calls us to worship saying, 'O magnify the Lord
with me, and let us exalt his name together' (Psalm 34:3).

In this we do no more than give the glory to God that is due
his name.

Andrew Murray (1828–1917)

The majesty of the creator God

This psalm lifts us up out of the mundane and praises God as creator of all things. It points clearly to the glory of God as seen in the starry skies. Here too is a note of deep wonder at God's condescension that he cares for frail humanity.

O LORD, our Sovereign,
how majestic is your name in all the earth!

You have set your glory above the heavens.
Out of the mouths of babes and infants
you have founded a bulwark because of your foes,
to silence the enemy and the avenger.

When I look at your heavens, the work of your fingers,
the moon and the stars that you have established;
what are human beings that you are mindful of them,
mortals that you care for them?

Yet you have made them a little lower than God,
and crowned them with glory and honour.
You have given them dominion over the works of your
hands;
you have put all things under their feet,
all sheep and oxen,
and also the beasts of the field,
the birds of the air, and the fish of the sea,
whatever passes along the paths of the seas.

O LORD, our Sovereign,
how majestic is your name in all the earth!

Psalm 8, NRSV

Make a joyful noise

One of the most common commands of the Bible is the call to worship and to sing in praise of God. Psalm 100 has been taken as the theme of a number of modern worship songs and its words also form part of the spoken liturgy in some church services.

Make a joyful noise to the LORD, all the earth.
Worship the Lord with gladness;
come into his presence with singing.

Know that the LORD is God.
It is he that made us, and we are his;
we are his people, and the sheep of his pasture.

Enter his gates with thanksgiving,
and his courts with praise.
Give thanks to him, bless his name.

For the LORD is good;
his steadfast love endures for ever,
and his faithfulness to all generations.

Psalm 100, NRSV

Man is but a reed

Blaise Pascal was a mathematician who devoted the last eight years of his life to philosophy and theology. This extract speaks not only of the weakness of human beings but also of our dignity and honour.

Man is but a reed, the most feeble thing in nature, but he is a thinking reed. The entire universe need not arm itself to crush him. A vapour, a drop of water suffices to kill him. But, if the universe were to crush him, man would still be more noble than that which killed him, because he knows that he dies and the advantage which the universe has over him, the universe knows nothing of this ... All our dignity then, consists in thought. By it we must elevate ourselves, and not by space and time which we cannot fill. Let us endeavour then, to think well; this is the principle of morality.

Blaise Pascal (1623–1662)

Man's equal

Matthew Henry was an English non-conformist clergyman who turned to theology after studying law. He is best known for his extensive commentary on the Bible. Here he comments on part of the creation story.

The woman was made of a rib out of the side of Adam; not made out of his head to rule over him, not out of his feet to be trampled on by him; but out of his side to be equal to him, under his arm to be protected, and near his heart to be loved.

Matthew Henry (1662–1714)

Man's purpose is to be happy

Kahlil Gibran, a poet, artist and writer, was born in Lebanon but spent most of his life in America. He is the third best-selling poet in history, after Shakespeare and Lao Tse.

Vain are the beliefs and teachings that make man miserable, and false is the goodness that leads him into sorrow and despair, for it is man's purpose to be happy on this earth and lead the way to felicity and preach its gospel wherever he goes. He who does not see the kingdom of heaven in this life will never see it in the coming life. We came not into this life by exile, but we came as innocent creatures of God, to learn how to worship the holy and eternal spirit and seek the hidden secrets within ourselves from the beauty of life. This is the truth which I have learned from the teachings of the Nazarene.

Kahlil Gibran (1883–1931)

Marks of a Christian

In addition to his work as a theologian, Basil of Caesarea was known for his care of the poor and underprivileged. He established guidelines for monastic life which focus on community life, liturgical prayer and manual labour. He is considered a saint by the traditions of both Eastern and Western Christianity. In this extract Basil identifies those things that should distinguish a Christian.

What is the distinguishing mark of a Christian? Faith working by love. What is the mark of faith? Unhesitating conviction of the truth of the inspired words, unshaken by any argument either based on the plea of physical necessity or masquerading in the guise of piety.

What is the mark of a believer? To hold fast by such conviction in the strength of what scripture says and to dare neither to set it at nought nor to add to it. For if what is not of faith is sin, as the apostle says, and faith comes from hearing and hearing through the word of God, then everything that is outside scripture, being not of faith, is sin.

What is the mark of love towards God? Keeping his commandments with a view to his glory. What is the mark of love towards our neighbour? Not to seek one's own good, but the good of the loved one for the benefit of his soul and body.

What is the mark of a Christian? To be born anew in baptism of water and Spirit. What is the mark of one who is born of water? As Christ died to sin once, that he should be thus dead and unmoved by any sin ... What is the mark of the one who is born of the Spirit? That he should be, according to the measure given him, that very thing of which he was born ...

What is the mark of the one who is born again? To put off the old man with his doings and lusts, and to put on the new man, which is being renewed unto knowledge after the image of him that created him ...

What is the mark of those who eat the bread and drink the cup of the Lord? To keep in perpetual memory him who died for us and rose again. What is the mark of those who keep such a memory? To live for themselves no longer, but unto him who died for them and rose again ...

What is the mark of the Christian? To love one another, even as Christ also loved us.

Basil of Caesarea (c. 329–379)

Marriage blessing

The following blessing is from the Syrian Orthodox Church. Syrian Christians placed great emphasis on the humility of Jesus and there were a number of great spiritual writers in the Syrian Church.

May God by whose will the world and all creation have their being, and who wills the life of all men – may Christ, the true bridegroom, seal your marriage in the truth of his love. As he finds joy in his Church, so may you find your happiness in one another; that your union may abound in love and your coming together in purity. May his angel guide you, may his peace reign between you, that in all things you may be guarded and guided, so that you may give thanks to the Father who will bless you, the Son who will rejoice in you, and the Spirit who will protect you, now and for ever and world without end.

Syrian Orthodox

Mary's song

Mary has been visited by the angel Gabriel, who has announced that she is to give birth to a child who will be the Son of God. She goes to visit her cousin Elizabeth, who is old and was said to be barren but is now also expecting a child. On Mary's arrival, the child in Elizabeth's womb leaps and Elizabeth declares that Mary is to be the mother of the Lord. Mary's song in response is known as the Magnificat.

And Mary said,
'My soul magnifies the Lord,
    and my spirit rejoices in God my Saviour,
for he has looked with favour on the lowliness of his servant.
    Surely, from now on all generations will call me blessed;
for the Mighty One has done great things for me,
    and holy is his name.
His mercy is for those who fear him
    from generation to generation.
He has shown strength with his arm;
    he has scattered the proud in the thoughts of their hearts.
He has brought down the powerful from their thrones,
    and lifted up the lowly;
he has filled the hungry with good things,
    and sent the rich away empty.
He has helped his servant Israel,
    in remembrance of his mercy,
according to the promise he made to our ancestors,
    to Abraham and to his descendants for ever.'

Luke 1:46–55, NRSV

May God shield us

At a time when pilgrimages were both common and potentially dangerous there might be a special service or ceremony before their departure. Prayers like this would be said, seeking God's protection and safekeeping.

May God shield us by each sheer drop,
May Christ keep us on each rock-path,
May the Spirit fill us on each bare slope, as we cross hill and
plain,
Who live and reign One God for ever.
Amen.

Anon.

Meek and lowly

Richard Baxter was an English Puritan church leader and theologian. He was ordained in the Church of England in his mid-twenties. He later served as chaplain to the Parliamentary troops during the Civil War but nevertheless supported the Restoration and was made a royal chaplain to King Charles II. Despite poor health, his later years were his most productive. Despite a career in which he mixed with royalty he here declares that humility is an essential feature of the Christian.

Humility is not a mere ornament of a Christian, but an essential part of the new creature. It is a contradiction to be a true Christian and not humble. All that will be Christians must be Christ's disciples and come to him to learn, and their lesson is to be 'meek and lowly'.

Richard Baxter (1615–1691)

The miracle of the radish

William Jennings Bryan was an American politician, speaker and lawyer. He is remembered today as an opponent of Darwinism; the following quote from him is a reminder of just how miraculous are the workings of nature that we so easily take for granted.

Some sceptics say, 'Oh, the miracles. I can't accept miracles.' Well consider this then. One may drop a brown seed in the black soil and up comes a green shoot. You let it grow and soon enough you'll pull up a root that is red. Now you cut that red root and you find it has a white heart. Can anyone tell me how this comes about – how brown cast into black turns up green with red underneath and white inside? Yet you eat your radish without even thinking of it as a miracle ... Everyday is a miracle – a miracle of life that sustains our hope!

William Jennings Bryan (1860–1925)

A morning prayer

Nerses Shnorhali, or 'Nerses the Graceful', was supreme Patriarch of Armenia between 1166 and 1173. He was a theologian, poet and composer, and wrote the following prayers for the sunrise, or Prime, service of the Armenian Church.

O light, Creator of Light; Primeval Light; who dwells in inaccessible light; O Heavenly Father, blessed by the orders of the shining angels at the dawn of this morning's light; shed forth into our souls your spiritual light.

Of Light from Light: Sun of Righteousness, Son of the Father, who is the Ineffable Offspring, whose name is hymned with the Father before the rising of the sun at dawn of this morning's light: shed forth into our souls your spiritual light.

O Light proceeding from the Father: you Holy Spirit: God, Fountain of Goodness: the children of the Church together with the angels praise you at the dawn of this morning's light: shed forth into our souls your spiritual light.

O Light Triune: Indivisible Holy Trinity, we sons of earth, together with the heavenly ones, ever glorify you at the dawn of the morning's light: shed forth into our souls your spiritual light.

Nerses Shnorhali (1100–1173)

Moses and the glory of the Lord

*While Moses is on the mountain top receiving God's laws, the people below
make a golden calf as an idol to worship. In his anger God declares that he
will not go with them but that they are to go to the Promised Land. Moses,
however, pleads with God, who speaks with him 'face to face', and God says
that he will, after all, go with the people. Moses then asks to see God's glory.*

Moses said, 'Show me your glory, I pray.' And he said, 'I will
make all my goodness pass before you, and will proclaim before
you the name, "The Lord"; and I will be gracious to whom I will
be gracious, and will show mercy on whom I will show mercy.
But', he said, 'you cannot see my face; for no one shall see me
and live.' And the Lord continued, 'See, there is a place by me
where you shall stand on the rock; and while my glory passes by
I will put you in a cleft of the rock, and I will cover you with my
hand until I have passed by; then I will take away my hand, and
you shall see my back; but my face shall not be seen.'

Exodus 33:18–23, NRSV

Motorist's prayer

This prayer, whose author is unknown, reminds us that when we drive may, if we do not pay attention carefully, either cause an accident or fail to appreciate all that is around us on our journey.

Grant me a road and a watchful eye,
That none may suffer hurts as I pass by;
Thou givest life – I pray no act of mine
May take away or mar that gift of thine.
Shield those, dear Lord, who bear me company
From fools and fire and all calamity.
Teach me to use my car for others' need,
Nor miss through lack of wit or love of speed
The beauties of thy world, that thus I may,
With joy and courtesy, go on my way.

Anon.

My colours

This passage was written by a young Zimbabwean pastor and it was found among his papers after he was martyred, shortly after its writing. The man who wrote it clearly knew what it meant to live in this way, and the things he wrote were true about his life. This passage could well be described as a mission statement for a disciple.

I am part of the fellowship of the unashamed. I have the Holy Spirit power. The die has been cast. I have stepped over the line. The decision has been made. I'm a disciple of his and I won't look back, let up, slow down, back away, or be still.

My past is redeemed. My present makes sense. My future is secure. I'm done and finished with low living, sight walking, small planning, smooth knees, colourless dreams, tamed visions, mundane talking, cheap living and dwarfed goals.

I no longer need pre-eminence, prosperity, position, promotions, plaudits, or popularity. I don't have to be right, or first, or tops, or recognised, or praised, or rewarded. I live by faith, lean on his presence, walk by patience, lift by prayer and labour by Holy Spirit power.

My face is set. My gait is fast. My goal is heaven. My road may be narrow, my way rough, my companions few, but my guide is reliable and my mission is clear.

I will not be bought, compromised, detoured, lured away, turned back, deluded or delayed.

I will not flinch in the face of sacrifice or hesitate in the presence of the adversary. I will not negotiate at the table of the enemy, ponder at the pool of popularity, or meander in the maze of mediocrity.

I won't give up, shut up, or let up until I have stayed up, stored up, prayed up, paid up, and preached up for the cause of Christ.

I am a disciple of Jesus. I must give until I drop, preach until all know, and work until he comes. And when he does come for his own, he'll have no problems recognising me.

My colours will be clear!

Anon.

My Master's face

In this poem, by nineteenth-century poet William Hurd Hillyer, we are reminded that although we have no physical record from his own time of what Christ looked like, and nothing written in his own hand, we can see him mirrored in the actions and words of those who are his followers.

No pictured likeness of my Lord
I have;
He carved no record
of his ministry
on wood or stone,
He left no sculptured tomb
nor parchment dim
but trusted for all memory of him
the heart alone.
Who sees the face but sees in part;
Who reads the spirit which it hides,
sees all;
he needs no more.
Thy life in my life, Lord,
give Thou to me;
and then, in truth,
I may forever see
my Master's face!

William Hurd Hillyer (1880 – ?)

My yoke is easy

This saying of Jesus from Matthew 11 is very well known, but a consideration of the context provides more insight into Jesus' message to his listeners. A yoke is invariably used by two animals rather than one – so in taking on Christ's yoke we are assured that he is bearing it alongside us; it is never something we have to carry alone.

'Come to me, all you that are weary and are carrying heavy burdens, and I will give you rest. Take my yoke upon you, and learn from me; for I am gentle and humble in heart, and you will find rest for your souls. For my yoke is easy, and my burden is light.'

Matthew 11:28–30, NRSV

Nature acknowledges God

John Clare was an English poet who rose from a very poor background to relative prosperity as a published and famous poet. However, he became an alcoholic and later suffered from depression. He spent his last twenty years in a Northamptonshire lunatic asylum, but nevertheless wrote some of his best-known poetry during this time.

All nature owns with one accord
The great and universal Lord;
The sun proclaims him through the day,
The moon when daylight drops away,
The very darkness smiles to wear
The stars that show us God is there,
On moonlight seas soft gleams the sky,
And 'God is with us' waves reply.

Winds breathe from God's abode, 'We come,'
Storms louder own God is their home,
And thunder yet with louder call,
Sounds, 'God is mightiest over all';
Till earth, right loath the proof to miss,
Echoes triumphantly 'He is,'
And air and ocean makes reply,
'God reigns on earth, in air and sky.'

All nature owns with one accord
The great and universal Lord:
Insect and bird and tree and flower –
The witnesses of every hour –
Are pregnant with his prophecy
And 'God is with us', all reply.
The first link in the mighty plan
Is still – and all upbraideth man.

John Clare (1793–1864)

The nature of love

Kahlil Gibran, a poet, artist and writer, was born in Lebanon but spent most of his life in America. This extract is a meditation on love: its relationship with God and also its fresh yet sensitive expression.

Love gives naught but itself and takes naught but from itself. Love possesses not nor would it be possessed. For love is sufficient unto love.

When you love you should not say, 'God is in my heart', but rather, 'I am in the heart of God.' And think not you can direct the course of love, for love, if it finds you worthy, directs your course.

Love has no other desire but to fulfil itself. But if you love and must needs have desires, let these be your desires: To melt and be like a running brook that sings its melody to the night. To know the pain of too much tenderness. To be wounded by your own understanding of love; And to bleed willingly and joyfully. To wake at dawn with a winged heart and give thanks for another day of loving; To rest at the noon hour and meditate love's ecstasy; to return home at eventide with gratitude; And then to sleep with a prayer for the beloved in your heart and a song of praise upon your lips.

Kahlil Gibran (1883–1931)

Necessary for understanding

Origen is generally considered the greatest theologian and biblical scholar of the early Eastern church. He was probably born in Egypt, perhaps in Alexandria, to a Christian family. Origen's literary productivity was enormous. His works include letters, treatises in dogmatic and practical theology, apologetics, exegeses and textual criticism. His writings helped to create a Christian theology that blended biblical and philosophical study.

What is most necessary for understanding divine things is prayer.

Origen (c. 185–254)

New heaven and new earth

In the book of Revelation, John describes visions of what life will be like when the end of this world as we know it has come and Christ rules over a new heaven and a new earth.

Then the angel showed me the river of the water of life, bright as crystal, flowing from the throne of God and of the Lamb through the middle of the street of the city. On either side of the river is the tree of life with its twelve kinds of fruit, producing its fruit each month; and the leaves of the tree are for the healing of the nations. Nothing accursed will be found there any more. But the throne of God and of the Lamb will be in it, and his servants will worship him; they will see his face, and his name will be on their foreheads. And there will be no more night; they need no light of lamp or sun, for the Lord God will be their light, and they will reign for ever and ever.

Revelation 22:1–5, NRSV

The new year

The new year is often seen as a time for thinking about new beginnings and resolving not to repeat the errors of the past. At this time it is also good to remember the source of all that is good in our lives and to thank God for what he provides day by day.

Bless us, O Lord, in this coming year.
May dew and rain be a source of blessing.
Bless to our use the fruits of the earth
And let the earth rejoice in them.
And bless all that we do
And the work of our hands.

Jewish prayer

No man is an island

John Donne was ordained in 1615 after a career in public service. Just six years later he became dean of St Paul's, where his preaching attracted large congregations. While he had been a poet before ordination he wrote prose in the years afterwards.

No man is an island, entire of itself; every man is a piece of the continent, a part of the main. If a clod be washed away by the sea, Europe is the less, as well as if a promontory were, as well as if a manor of thy friend's or of thine own were; Any man's death diminishes me, because I am involved in mankind; And therefore never send to know for whom the bell tolls; it tolls for thee.

John Donne (1572–1631)

No mere religion

William Stringfellow was born in Johnston, Rhode Island, USA. He managed to gain several scholarships and a place to study at Bates College by the age of fifteen. Another scholarship took him to the London School of Economics. It was here, he was to write later, that he learned the difference between vocation and career. Later he went to Harvard Law School. He had a passion for social justice and went to work as a lawyer in Harlem, New York. Knowing that his Lord had touched the untouchable – lepers – he represented victimized tenants, those who would otherwise have inadequate counsel in the courts, and impoverished black people who were shut out of public services like hospitals and government offices. After his death it was said of him that, 'In his vocation and by his example he opened up to us the Word of God.'

Personally I find no cause to be interested in mere religion. It can be a certain diversion, I admit, to speculate and argue about religious ideas and practices, but ... it appears to me more urgent and more necessary to deal with history, that is, with actual life as it has preceded the present time, and with the actual life of the present time. So I do not bother, as far as I am aware, with dabbling in religion.

... But when, now and then, I turn to and listen to the Bible, or when, now and then, I hear the Word of God exposed in preaching, or when, now and then, I see the gospel represented in the Holy Communion and I thereupon become a participant in and witness of the real life that is given to the world, or when, now and then, I meet some Christian, or when, now and then, I discern and encounter the presence of God's Word in the ordinary affairs of everyday existence in the world – on these occasions, in these circumstances, I am reminded, if sometimes ruefully, that the gospel is no mere religion in *any* essential respect.

William Stringfellow (1928–1985)

Not reading, but doing

Thomas à Kempis was a Catholic monk, his best-known work is The Imitation of Christ. *This brief quotation is a reminder that our actions are all-important.*

At the Day of Judgement we shall not be asked what we have read but what we have done.

Thomas à Kempis (c. 1380–1471)

Not to criticise

Oswald Chambers here encourages us, instead of finding fault with people, to bring them before God in prayer. Chambers was a Scottish Christian minister and teacher, best known as the author of the devotional book My Utmost for His Highest. *He died while serving as a chaplain during the First World War.*

God never allows us to see another person at fault so we may criticise them, but only that we might intercede.

Oswald Chambers (1874–1917)

O little Bethlehem

Bernard of Clairvaux was a French abbot and a founder of the Cistercian Order, which had begun as a community of reformed Benedictines at Citeaux. When this community grew too large, it planted new communities and Clairvaux was founded in 1115 with Bernard appointed as its abbot. This quotation reminds us of the value the Lord places on what is insignificant from a human point of view.

Not in the royal city of Jerusalem was Jesus born, but in Bethlehem, which is the least among the thousands of Judah. O little Bethlehem, made glorious by the Lord, even by him who, though great, in thee was made little! Rejoice, O Bethlehem, and through all thy streets let the festal hallelujah be sung.

Bernard of Clairvaux (1091–1153)

Obedience

John Calvin was a French Protestant theologian at the time of the Protestant Reformation. He was such an important figure at that time that the Reformed theology developed then is also known as Calvinism. He is particularly known for writing Institutes of the Christian Religion.

All true knowledge of God is born out of obedience.

John Calvin (1509–1564)

Observe good faith

George Washington, the first President of the United States, made his farewell speech to the American public on 17 September 1796. In it, he summarized his political ideas and each year the speech in full is read in both the Senate and the House of Representatives, to remind the nation of his political beliefs.

Observe good faith and justice towards all nations; cultivate peace and harmony with all; religion and morality enjoin this conduct; and can it be that good policy does not equally enjoin it? It will be worthy of a free, enlightened, and at no distant period, a great nation, to give to mankind the magnanimous and too novel example of a people always guided by an exalted justice and benevolence. Who can doubt that, in the course of time and things, the fruits of such a plan would richly repay any temporary advantages which might be lost by a steady adherence to it? Can it be that Providence has not connected the permanent felicity of a nation with its virtue. The experiment, at least, is recommended by every sentiment which ennobles human nature. Alas! is it rendered impossible by its vices?

George Washington (1732–1799)

Observing the Lord's Day

Matthew Hale studied to become a Christian minister but changed his mind and pursued a legal career, eventually becoming Lord Chief Justice of England. He was known for his devotion and his diligent and determined independence in his legal judgments.

I have found by a strict and diligent observation that a due observance of the duties of the Lord's Day has always had joined to it a blessing on the rest of my time, and the week that has been so begun has been blessed and prosperous to me. On the other side, when I have been negligent of the duties of the day, the rest of the week has been unsuccessful and unhappy in my own secular employments. I write this, not lightly or inconsiderately, but upon long and sound observation and experience.

Sir Matthew Hale (1609–1676)

On the Damascus road

People come to faith in many different ways: some are brought up in believing households and, without being able to put a date to it, realize at some point that they have adopted these beliefs for themselves. Others undergo a more identifiable conversion experience and can recall the time and place that they first believed. This latter is often called a 'Damascus road' experience because of the dramatic way in which Saul, later called Paul, met personally with Jesus Christ.

Meanwhile Saul, still breathing threats and murder against the disciples of the Lord, went to the high priest and asked him for letters to the synagogues at Damascus, so that if he found any who belonged to the Way, men or women, he might bring them bound to Jerusalem. Now as he was going along and approaching Damascus, suddenly a light from heaven flashed around him. He fell to the ground and heard a voice saying to him, 'Saul, Saul, why do you persecute me?' He asked, 'Who are you, Lord?' The reply came, 'I am Jesus, whom you are persecuting. But get up and enter the city, and you will be told what you are to do.' The men who were travelling with him stood speechless because they heard the voice but saw no one. Saul got up from the ground, and though his eyes were open, he could see nothing; so they led him by the hand and brought him into Damascus. For three days he was without sight, and neither ate nor drank.

Now there was a disciple in Damascus named Ananias. The Lord said to him in a vision, 'Ananias.' He answered, 'Here I am, Lord.' The Lord said to him, 'Get up and go to the street called Straight, and at the house of Judas look for a man of Tarsus named Saul. At this moment he is praying, and he has seen in a vision a man named Ananias come in and lay his hands on him so that he might regain his sight.' But Ananias answered, 'Lord, I have heard from many about this man, how much evil he has done to your saints in Jerusalem; and here he has authority from the chief priests to bind all who invoke your name.' But the Lord said to him, 'Go, for he is an instrument whom I have chosen to bring my name before Gentiles and kings and before the people of Israel; I myself will show him how much he must suffer for the sake of my name.' So Ananias went and entered the house. He laid his hands on Saul and said, 'Brother Saul, the Lord Jesus, who appeared to you on your way here, has sent me so that you may regain your sight and be filled with the Holy Spirit.' And immediately something like scales fell from his eyes, and his sight was restored. Then he got up and was baptized, and after taking some food, he regained his strength.

Acts 9:1–19, NRSV

Only sinners need forgiveness

John Wesley was an eighteenth-century preacher and a founder of Methodism. He evangelized widely, especially in the open air. His early education was largely undertaken by his mother Susanna, who was a very significant influence on her children.

Who are they that are justified? The ungodly – the ungodly of every kind and degree, and none but the ungodly. It is only sinners that have any occasion for pardon; it is sin alone which admits of being forgiven. Forgiveness has an immediate reference to sin, and to nothing else. It is our unrighteousness to which the pardoning Lord is merciful; it is our iniquity that he remembers no more.

John Wesley (1703–1791)

Opening the door to Christ

John Stott is a Christian leader and Anglican clergyman noted as a leader of the worldwide evangelical movement. While he was a teenager at Rugby School, a preacher pointed John to Revelation 3:20, 'Behold, I stand at the door, and knock: if any man hear my voice, and open the door, I will come in to him, and will sup with him, and he with me.' Stott later described the impact this verse had upon him.

Here, then, is the crucial question which we have been leading up to. Have we ever opened our door to Christ? Have we ever invited him in? This was exactly the question which I needed to have put to me. For, intellectually speaking, I had believed in Jesus all my life, on the other side of the door. I had regularly struggled to say my prayers through the key-hole. I had even pushed pennies under the door in a vain attempt to pacify him. I had been baptised, yes and confirmed as well. I went to church, read my Bible, had high ideals, and tried to be good and do good. But all the time, often without realising it, I was holding Christ at arm's length, and keeping him outside. I knew that to open the door might have momentous consequences. I am profoundly grateful to him for enabling me to open the door. Looking back now over more than fifty years, I realise that that simple step has changed the entire direction, course and quality of my life.

John Stott, quoted in Timothy Dudley-Smith's
The Making of a Leader (IVP, 1999)

Peace of mind

Howard Thurman was an American writer, philosopher, civil-rights leader and theologian. He was ordained as a Baptist minister in 1925 and went on to write many books. He was a classmate and friend of Martin Luther King Sr, and mentored Martin Luther King Jr when he was at Boston University.

'Seek ye first the rule of God,' the Master says. And after that? The key that one needs for one's peace is in the heart. There can be no personal freedom where there is not an initial personal surrender.

Howard Thurman (1899–1981)

The pearl of great price

John Mason was known as a pious, learned man and a good parish priest. He acquired a nation-wide reputation as a prolific hymn-writer and was the direct ancestor of the very well-known nineteenth-century hymn-writer and translator John Mason Neale. Jesus likened the kingdom of heaven to a pearl of great price (Matthew 13:45–46).

I've found the pearl of greatest price,
My heart doth sing for joy;
And sing I must, for Christ is mine,
Christ shall my song employ.

Christ is my Prophet, Priest, and King;
My Prophet full of light,
My great High Priest before the throne,
My King of heavenly might.

For he indeed is Lord of lords,
And he the King of kings;
He is the Sun of Righteousness,
With healing in his wings.

Christ is my peace; he died for me,
For me he shed his blood;
And as my wondrous sacrifice,
Offered himself to God.

Christ Jesus is my All-in-all,
My comfort and my love,
My life below, and he shall be
My glory-crown above.

John Mason (c. 1645–1694)

A people for God

God has called Abraham to follow him and to be the father of a great nation. Abraham has believed God's promises and, before assuring him that he and Sarah will indeed have a child, God makes a covenant with Abraham.

I will establish my covenant between me and you, and your offspring after you throughout their generations, for an everlasting covenant, to be God to you and to your offspring after you. And I will give to you, and to your offspring after you, the land where you are now an alien, all the land of Canaan, for a perpetual holding; and I will be their God.

God said to Abraham, 'As for you, you shall keep my covenant, you and your offspring after you throughout their generations.'

Genesis 17:7–9, NRSV

Persistence

Baron Friedrich Von Hügel was born in Italy to an Austrian father and Scottish mother. He moved to England with his family in 1867 and remained there for the rest of his life, becoming a naturalized Englishman in 1914 after the outbreak of the First World War. He was a Roman Catholic lay philosopher and writer and reminds us that the worthwhile things in life, the real achievements, are not gained in fits and starts, but by persistent effort and sacrifice.

Experienced mountaineers have a quiet, regular, short step – on the level it looks petty; but in this step they keep up, on and on as they ascend, whilst the inexperienced townsman hurries along, and soon has to stop, dead beat with the climb ... Such an expert mountaineer, when the thick mists come, halts and camps out under some slight cover brought with him, quietly smoking his pipe, and moving on only when the mist has cleared away ... You want to grow in virtue, to serve God, to love Christ? Well you will grow in and attain to these things if you will make them a slow and sure, an utterly real, a mountain step-plod and ascent, willing to have to camp for weeks or months in spiritual desolation, darkness and emptiness, at different stages in your march and growth. All demand for constant light, for ever the best, all attempt at eliminating or minimizing the cross and trial, is so much soft folly and puerile trifling.

Baron Friedrich von Hügel (1852–1925)

Pilgrim's Progress

It was said that for two hundred years most homes in England contained not just the King James Version *of the Bible, but a copy of John Bunyan's* The Pilgrim's Progress. *Written while he was in prison after the restoration of the monarchy in 1660, the story portrays the journey of life. Here, Christian and Hopeful face death.*

Then said Christian, 'Ah, my friend, the sorrows of death have compassed me about; I shall not see the land that flows with milk and honey' ... Then said Hopeful, ... 'These troubles and distresses that you go through in these waters are no sign that God hath forsaken you; but are sent to try you whether you will call to mind that which heretofore you have received of his goodness, and live upon him in your distresses' ... And with that Christian broke out with a loud voice, 'Oh, I see him again! And he tells me, "When thou passest through the waters, I will be with thee ..."'

John Bunyan (1628–1688)

Polycarp's prayer

Saint Polycarp was a Christian bishop of Smyrna (now Izmir in Turkey) in the second century. He was stabbed to death as a martyr after an attempt to burn him at the stake failed. Polycarp is recognized as a saint in both the Roman Catholic and Eastern Orthodox churches.

Lord God Almighty, Father of your beloved and blessed Son Jesus Christ, through whom we have received knowledge of you, God of angels and powers, of the whole creation and of the whole race of the righteous who live in your sight, I bless you, for having made me worthy of this day and hour, I bless you, because I may have a part, along with the martyrs, in the chalice of your Christ, to resurrection in eternal life, resurrection both of soul and body in the incorruptibility of the Holy Spirit. May I be received today, as a rich and acceptable sacrifice, among those who are in you presence, as you have prepared and foretold and fulfilled, God who is faithful and true. For this and for all benefits I praise you, I bless you, I glorify you, through the eternal and heavenly High Priest, Jesus Christ, your beloved Son, through whom be to you with him and the Holy Spirit glory, now and for all the ages to come. Amen.

Polycarp (c. 69–c. 155)

Praise God, from whom all blessings flow

Thomas Ken was born in Hertfordshire in 1637. He was a chaplain to King Charles II, appointed to be a bishop in the Church of England in 1684 and was and one of the fathers of modern English hymn writing. He had a fine combination of spiritual insight and feeling with poetic taste, which marks all great hymn writers. This expression of praise celebrates who God is and what he has done.

Praise God, from whom all blessings flow;
Praise him, all creatures here below;
Praise him above, you heavenly host;
Praise Father, Son and Holy Ghost.

Thomas Ken (1637–1711)

Pray anyway

Julian of Norwich is considered to be one of the greatest English mystics. Little is known of her life except her writings. Although she lived in a time of turmoil, her theology was optimistic, speaking of God's love in terms of joy and compassion as opposed to law and duty. She did not see suffering as a punishment that God inflicted; her theology was that God loved and saved us all.

Pray inwardly, even if you do not enjoy it. It does good though you feel nothing, even though you think you are doing nothing.

Julian of Norwich (c. 1342–c. 1416)

The prayer

Jones Very was an American poet and clergyman who produced just one book of poetry. He did not become well known but was regarded as something of a mystic during his lifetime.

Wilt thou not visit me?
The plant beside me feels thy gentle dew,
And every blade of grass I see
From thy deep earth its quickening moisture drew.

Wilt thou not visit me?
Thy morning calls on me with cheering tone;
And every hill and tree
Lend but one voice – the voice of thee alone.

Come, for I need thy love,
More than the flower the dew or grass the rain;
Come, gently as thy holy dove;
And let me in thy sight rejoice to live again.

I will not hide from them
When thy storms come, though fierce may be their wrath,
But bow with leafy stem,
And strengthened follow on thy chosen path.

Yes, thou wilt visit me:
Nor plant nor tree thine eye delights so well,
As when from sin set free,
My spirit loves with thine in peace to dwell.

Jones Very (1813–1880)

Prayer for humility

William Barclay was a twentieth-century author, minister in the Church of Scotland and academic. As Professor of Divinity and Biblical Criticism in Glasgow, he dedicated his life to 'making the best biblical scholarship available to the average reader'. The following extract is from his commentary on John's Gospel.

O Father, give us the humility which
    Realises its ignorance,
    Admits its mistakes,
    Recognises its need,
    Welcomes advice,
    Accepts rebuke.
Help us always
    To praise rather than to criticise,
    To sympathise rather than to condemn,
    To encourage rather than to discourage,
    To build rather than to destroy,
    And to think of people at their best rather than at their
        worst.
This we ask for thy name's sake.

William Barclay (1907–1978)

Prayer for mourners

This prayer is taken from the Catholic Family Prayer Book *and is particularly for those who have lost a child.*

Lord God,
You are attentive to the voice of our pleading.
Let us find in your Son
Comfort in our sadness,
Certainty in our doubts,
And courage to live through this hour.
Make our faith strong
Through Christ.
O Lord,
Whose ways are beyond understanding,
Listen to the prayers of your faithful people:
That those weighed down by grief at the loss of this child
May find reassurance in your infinite goodness.
We ask this through Christ our Lord.
Amen.

Anon.

Prayer for peace

Alan Paton was a South African teacher who objected to the apartheid legislation in that country, and founded the South African Liberal Party to oppose it. Unlike some members of the party, he was noted for his peaceful opposition. He wrote a number of novels, the best-known of which is Cry, the Beloved Country, *dealing with the racial situation in South Africa.*

O Lord, open my eyes
That I may see the needs of others,
Open my ears that I may hear their cries,
Open my heart so that they need not be without success.
Let me not be afraid to defend the weak
Because of the anger of the strong,
Nor afraid to defend the poor
Because of the anger of the rich.
Show me where love and hope and faith are needed,
And use me to bring them to those places.
Open my eyes and ears that I may, this coming day,
Be able to do some work of peace for thee.

Alan Paton (1903–1988)

The Prayer of St Francis

Francis of Assisi was a Roman Catholic friar and founder of the Franciscan Order. The Prayer of St Francis is a Christian prayer for peace, and although attributed to St Francis of Assisi it can only be traced back as far as its first appearance in 1912. This is a modern version, which has been set to music.

Make me a channel of your peace
Where there is hatred let me bring your love.
Where there is injury, your pardon Lord,
And where there is doubt, true faith in You.

Make me a channel of your peace.
Where there's despair in life let me bring hope.
Where there is darkness, only light
And where there's sadness only joy.

O Master grant that I may never seek
So much to be consoled as to console,
To be understood as to understand
To be loved as to love with all my soul.

Make me a channel of your peace
It is in pardoning that we are pardoned,
It is in giving to all men that we receive
And in dying that we are born to eternal life.

St Francis of Assisi (1181–1226)

Praying and trusting

Julian of Norwich was one of the great English mystics. Little is known about her life except her writings. Having narrowly survived death from illness at the age of 30 (purportedly through prayer) she fell seriously ill once more in 1373 and experienced a series of 16 revelatory visions, mostly concerning the passion of Christ. This meditation describes the presence of God surrounding our prayer.

Prayer is not overcoming God's reluctance. It is laying hold of his willingness. This is our Lord's will, ... that our prayer and our trust be, alike, large. For if we do not trust as much as we pray, we fail in full worship to our Lord in our prayer; and also we hinder and hurt ourselves. The reason is that we do not know truly that our Lord is the ground from which our prayer springs; nor do we know that it is given us by his grace and his love. If we knew this, it would make us trust to have of our Lord's gifts all that we desire. For I am sure that no man asks mercy and grace with sincerity, without mercy and grace being given to him first.

Julian of Norwich (c. 1342–c. 1416)

The presence of God

Brother Lawrence was a lay brother in a Carmelite monastery. He is best remembered today for writing the classic Christian text The Practice of the Presence of God. *These are the four spiritual principles that he urged Christian followers to observe.*

To look always to God and his glory in all that we do, say, and undertake; that the end we seek should be to become faultless worshippers of God in this life as we hope to be throughout eternity; firmly to resolve to overcome with God's grace all the difficulties which confront us in the spiritual life.

When we undertake the spiritual life, we must bear in mind who we are, and we shall realise that we are worthy of all scorn, unworthy of the name of Christian, subject to all manner of tribulations, or troublesome circumstances beyond number, which make us uneven in our health, moods and disposition of heart and of behaviour, in a word people whom God desires to bring low by countless trials and travail as much within as without.

We must without doubt believe that it is to our advantage, that it is pleasing to God to sacrifice us to himself, that it is the way of his Providence to allow us to face all manner of situations, to suffer all manner of afflictions and wretchedness, and temptations for the love of God, so long as it shall please him, since, without this submission of heart and spirit to the will of God, devotion and perfection cannot exist.

A soul is the more dependent upon grace according as it aspires to a higher perfection, and God's help is the more necessary at each moment, for without it, it can do nothing; the world, nature and the devil join in a conflict so strong and continuous, that without this present help, and this humble and necessary dependence, they will drag it away in spite of itself; this appears hard to nature but grace accepts it and rests in it.

Brother Lawrence (c. 1610–1691)

Prevailing prayer

Samuel Chadwick was born in the north of England, into a devout Methodist family. He became a lay pastor at the age of 21 and wrote a number of books. He became the principal of the Methodist training college, Cliff College in Derbyshire.

There is no power like that of prevailing prayer – of Abraham pleading for Sodom, Jacob wrestling in the stillness of the night, Moses standing in the breach, Hannah intoxicated with sorrow, David heartbroken with remorse and grief, Jesus in sweat of blood. Add to this list from the records of the church your personal observation and experience, and always there is cost of passion unto blood. Such prayer prevails. It turns ordinary mortals into men of power. It brings power. It brings fire. It brings rain. It brings life. It brings God.

Samuel Chadwick (1840–1932)

Problem solving

Peter Taylor Forsyth was a Scottish theologian, considered by some to be among the greatest English-speaking theologians of the early twentieth century

You must live with people to know their problems, and live with God in order to solve them.

P T Forsyth (1842–1921)

Protect our journey

Mary Batchelor is an English writer and a former teacher. She has compiled a number of anthologies of prayers and of Christian poetry. This Jewish prayer is designed for use before setting out on a journey.

O Lord our God and God of our fathers!
Mercifully direct and guide our steps to our destination and
    let us arrive there in health, joy and peace!
Keep us from all snares and dangers,
And protect us from any enemies that we might meet along
    the way.
Bless and protect our journey!
Let us win favour in your eyes and in the sight of those
    around us.
Blessed are you, O Lord,
Who hears and grants our prayers!

Anon.

Putting love into practice

Ignatius was born in Spain and decided to dedicate himself to a life of missionary work when, recovering from serious injury to his legs from a cannonball shot, he read religious books about the life of Jesus and the saints. He particularly admired Francis of Assisi. He went on to found the Jesuit Order and is best known for the Spiritual Exercises, *a set of meditations, prayers and other mental exercises.*

Love consists in sharing what one has
and what one is
with those one loves.
Love ought to show itself in deeds more than in words.

I ask the Father to give me an intimate knowledge
of the many gifts I have received,
that filled with gratitude for all,
I may in all things love and serve the Divine Majesty.

St Ignatius of Loyola (1491–1556)

A Quaker prayer

William Penn, a pacifist Quaker, was a champion of democracy and religious freedom. He was born in London and died in Berkshire but is perhaps best known as the founder of the province of Pennsylvania, which was an English colony but became the American state. The following prayer, ascribed to William Penn, is often used at funerals.

We give them back to thee, dear Lord, who gavest them to
    us;
Yet as thou dost not lose them in giving, so we have not lost
    them by their return.
Not as the world giveth, givest Thou, O Lover of Souls.
What thou gavest, Thou takest not away,
For what is thine is ours always if we are thine.
And Life is eternal and Love is immortal, and death is only
    an horizon,
And an horizon is nothing save the limit of our sight.
Lift us up, strong Son of God, that we may see further;
Cleanse our eyes that we may see more clearly;
And draw us closer to thyself that we may know ourselves
To be nearer to our loved ones who are with thee.
And while thou dost prepare for us, prepare us also for that
    happy place,
That where they are and thou art, we too may be for
    evermore.

William Penn (1644–1718)

Reading God's word

Kierkegaard was a Danish philosopher and theologian in the nineteenth century. His work spanned the disciplines of philosophy, theology, psychology and literature.

When you read God's word, you must constantly be saying to yourself, 'It is talking to me, and about me.'

Søren Kierkegaard (1813–1855)

Rejoice in the Lord

Paul concludes his letter to the church at Philippi by calling on them to demonstrate their following of Christ's teaching by expressing their joy in the Lord, loving one another, being faithful in prayer and concentrating on good things.

Rejoice in the Lord always; again I will say, Rejoice. Let your gentleness be known to everyone. The Lord is near. Do not worry about anything, but in everything by prayer and supplication with thanksgiving let your requests be made known to God. And the peace of God, which surpasses all understanding, will guard your hearts and your minds in Christ Jesus.

Finally, beloved, whatever is true, whatever is honourable, whatever is just, whatever is pure, whatever is pleasing, whatever is commendable, if there is any excellence and if there is anything worthy of praise, think about these things. Keep on doing the things that you have learned and received and heard and seen in me, and the God of peace will be with you.

Philippians 4:4–9, NRSV

The religion of joy

*Octavius Winslow was descended from a Pilgrim leader who braved the
Atlantic to travel to the New World on the* Mayflower *in 1620. Octavius's
father, Thomas, an army captain stationed in London, died when he was
seven years old. Shortly after that, Octavius's God-fearing mother took her
family of ten children to New York. All of the children became Christians,
and three sons became evangelical ministers.*

The religion of Christ is the religion of joy. Christ came to
take away our sins, to roll off our curse, to unbind our chains, to
open our prison house, to cancel our debt; in a word, to give us
the oil of joy for mourning, the garment of praise for the spirit of
heaviness. Is not this joy? Where can we find a joy so real, so
deep, so pure, so lasting? There is every element of joy – deep,
ecstatic, satisfying, sanctifying joy – in the gospel of Christ. The
believer in Jesus is essentially a happy man. The child of God is,
from necessity, a joyful man. His sins are forgiven, his soul is
justified, his person is adopted, his trials are blessings, his
conflicts are victories, his death is immortality, his future is a
heaven of inconceivable, unthought-of, untold, and endless
blessedness – with such a God, such a Saviour, and such a hope,
is he not, ought he not, to be a joyful man?

Octavius Winslow (1808–1878)

Resting-places

William Temple combined a strong social concern with a commitment to the spiritual life. He was Archbishop of York from 1928 to 1942 and then Archbishop of Canterbury until his death.

The Lord calls us to absolute perfection; but he points us here and now to what is for each one the next stage, the next resting-place, on the way to it. And as we follow, we find him there to welcome us. More than that – he comes to lead us there ... Our spiritual dragoman, who has gone forward to make preparation, returns to encourage us and lead us to the resting-place prepared. That resting-place is fellowship, fuller than before, with the Lord – that where I am ye also may be – until the last stage is reached, towards which we press on, 'the goal of the call upward which God gives in Christ Jesus'.

William Temple (1881–1944)

The resurrection of Christ

Wilbur Morehead Smith was born in Chicago. His parents were Presbyterians and Smith identified with this denomination all his life. His book Therefore Stand *created a sensation when it was published in 1945. It was a huge success and was described as 'the ablest defence of evangelical Christianity in many years'.*

The meaning of the resurrection is a theological matter, but the fact of the resurrection is a historical matter; the nature of the resurrection body of Jesus may be a mystery, but the fact that the body disappeared from the tomb is a matter to be decided upon by historical evidence.

Wilbur M Smith (1894–1977)

Rich in grace

Thomas à Kempis was a Catholic monk and author of The Imitation of Christ. *This extract is a reminder of the lives of earlier generations of believers who gave themselves tirelessly to God and others ... and they were sustained by fresh suppliers of divine aid and sustenance.*

Consider the spirited example of the holy Fathers ... Their whole time was spent fruitfully; every hour seemed short in the service of God; and by reason of the great delight they found in contemplation, they forgot the need for bodily refreshment. They renounced all riches, dignities, honours, friends and kinsfolk; they desired nothing which appertained to the world; they partook only of what was necessary for the sustenance of life; they were reluctant to serve the body even in necessity. They were poor in earthly things, but exceedingly rich in grace and all virtues. Outwardly they suffered want but inwardly they were refreshed with divine grace and consolation.

Thomas à Kempis (c. 1380–1471)

Richer than all men

John Chrysostom was a fourth-century bishop of Constantinople and early Church father. He emphasized charitable giving and was concerned with the spiritual and temporal needs of the poor. He also spoke out against abuse of wealth and personal property.

Do you wish to honour the body of Christ? Do not ignore him when he is naked. Do not pay him homage in the temple clad in silk, only then to neglect him outside where he is cold and ill-clad. He who said: 'This is my body' is the same who said: 'You saw me hungry and you gave me no food', and 'Whatever you did to the least of my brothers you did also to me' ... What good is it if the Eucharistic table is overloaded with golden chalices when your brother is dying of hunger? Start by satisfying his hunger and then with what is left you may adorn the altar as well.

John Chrysostom (c. 347–c. 407)

Risking love

There are a number of variations on the following saying, the author of which is unknown. However, they all carry the same message – that to live a full life it is necessary to take risks, and especially to take the risk of loving.

To love is to risk not being loved in return
To hope is to risk disappointment.
But risks must be taken because the greatest risk in life is to
risk nothing.
The person who risks nothing, does nothing, sees nothing,
has nothing and is nothing.
He cannot learn, feel, change, grow, love and live.

Anon.

Safe in God's hand

Columba was a sixth-century Gaelic missionary monk. He wrote several hymns, and the following is a verse from one of them. Columba died on Iona and was buried in the abbey he founded there.

Alone with none but thee, my God,
I journey on my way.
What need I fear, when thou art near
O King of night and day?
More safe am I within thy hand
Than if a host did round me stand.

St Columba (521–597)

Seeing God

Gregory of Nyssa was a fourth-century Christian bishop, the younger brother of Basil the Great and a friend of Gregory Nazianzus. Gregory and his two brothers, Basil and Peter, are known as the Cappadocian Fathers. Here he describes how following a Christian way of life, and seeking to be without sin, will help Christians to realize the truth that God is with them.

It is just like men who look at the sun in a mirror. Even though they do not look up directly at the heavens, they do see the sun in the mirror's reflection just as much as those who look directly at the sun. So it is, says our Lord, with you. Even though you are not strong enough to see the light itself, yet you will find within yourselves what you are seeking, if you will but return to the grace of that image which was established within you from the beginning. For the Godhead is all purity, freedom from passion, the absence of evil. And if you possess these qualities, God will surely be within you. When your mind is untainted by an evil, free of passion, purified of all stain, then you will be blessed because your eye is clear. Then, because you have been purified, you will perceive things that are invisible to the unpurified. The dark cloud of matter will be removed from the eye of your soul, and then you will see clearly that blessed vision within the pure brilliance of your own heart. And what is this vision? It is purity, holiness, simplicity, and other such brilliant reflections of the nature of God, for it is in these things that God is seen.

Gregory of Nyssa (330–c. 395)

Seeing more of God

Matthew Henry was an English non-conformist clergyman who turned to theology after studying law. He is best known for his extensive commentary on the Bible. Here he comments on Moses' prayer to see God's glory (Exodus 33:18).

Observe the humble request Moses makes: *I beseech thee, show me thy glory,* v. 18. Moses had just been on the mountain with God, had remained there a long time, and had enjoyed as intimate a communion with God as ever anyone had on this side of heaven, but he is still desiring further acquaintance. All who are effectually called to know God and fellowship with him still seek to know more and more of him, until they come to see as they are seen. Moses had wonderfully prevailed with God for one favour after another, and the success of his prayers made him bolder to go on and seek God further. The more he had, the more he asked. When we are in a good frame at the throne of grace, we should seek to preserve and make the most of it, and strike while the iron is hot: *"Show me thy glory; make me to see* it" (as the word is); "make it visible in some way or other, and enable me to bear the sight of it." Not that he was so ignorant as to think God's essence could be seen with physical eyes, but, having up to that time only heard a voice out of a pillar of cloud or fire, he desired to see some representation of divine glory, such as God saw fit to satisfy him with. It was not right that the people should see any form when the Lord spoke unto them, *lest they should corrupt themselves;* but he hoped there was not that danger in his seeing some form. Moses desired something more than he had seen up to that time. If it was purely to assist his faith and devotion, the desire was commendable, but perhaps there was in it a mixture of human infirmity. God wants us to walk by faith, not by sight, in this world, and *faith comes by hearing.* Some think that Moses wanted a sight of God's glory as a sign of his reconciliation, and as a pledge of the presence that he had promised them, but he did not know what he asked.

Matthew Henry (1662–1714)

Self-will

Louis de Blois, or Blosius as he is also known, was a sixteenth-century Flemish mystical writer. He joined a monastic Order at the age of fourteen and remained at the same monastery, of which he became abbot, until his death.

Self-will should be so completely poured out of the vessel of the soul into the ocean of the will of God, that whatever God may will, that at once the soul should will; and that whatever God may allow, that the soul should at once willingly embrace, whether it may be in itself sweet or bitter.

Louis de Blois (1506–1566)

The service of God

Sir Walter Raleigh was a famous soldier and explorer. He has been credited with bringing both potatoes and tobacco back to Britain, although both of these were already known via the Spanish. He was a courtier at the court of Queen Elizabeth I and later, while imprisoned in the Tower of London, wrote The History of the World. *He was beheaded at Whitehall having been accused of plotting against King James.*

The service of God is the path leading us to perfect happiness, and has in it a true, though not complete happiness; yielding such abundance of joy to the conscience, as doth easily counterbalance all afflictions whatsoever; though, indeed, those brambles that sometimes tear the skin off such as walk in this blessed way, do commonly lay hold upon them, at such time as they sit down to take their ease, and make them wish themselves at their journey's end, in the presence of their Lord, in whose presence is the fulness of joy.

Sir Walter Raleigh (1552–1618)

Serving

Mother Teresa was born in Albania and became a Roman Catholic nun. She founded the Missionaries of Charity in Calcutta in 1950. For over forty years she ministered to the poor and to outcasts, while overseeing the expansion of the work of the Missionaries of Charity, first throughout India and then in other countries. In 1979 she was awarded the Nobel Peace Prize.

If we pray
We will believe
If we believe
We will love
If we love
We will serve.
Only then can we put
Our love for God
Into living action
Through service of Christ
In the distressing
Disguise of the Poor.

    Mother Teresa (1910–1997)

Serving God

Ignatius was born in Spain and decided to dedicate himself to a life of missionary work when, recovering from serious injury to his legs from a cannonball shot, he read religious books about the life of Jesus and the saints. He particularly admired Francis of Assisi. He went on to found the Jesuit Order and is best known for the Spiritual Exercises, *a set of meditations, prayers and other mental exercises. This prayer focuses on the giving of ourselves to God and others rather than being preoccupied with ourselves.*

Dear Lord, teach me to be generous;
Teach me to serve you as you deserve;
To give and not to count the cost;
To fight and not to heed the wounds;
To toil, and not to seek for rest;
To labour, and not to ask for any reward,
Except that of knowing that I am doing your holy will.
Amen.

St Ignatius of Loyola (1491–1556)

Share the gospel

Francis of Assisi was a Roman Catholic friar and founder of the Franciscan Order. He is known as the patron saint of animals, birds and the environment because of his love for the natural world and stories of how he preached to birds and animals.

Share the gospel; if necessary, use words.
St Francis of Assisi (1181–1226)

Shout joyfully

Francis of Assisi began preaching in 1208 and received papal approval for the founding of his religious order in the following year. The last three years of his life were spent in solitude and prayer. He wrote a number of well-known prayers and poems, including the Canticle of the Sun.

Shout joyfully to God, all the earth,
Sing praise to his name,
Proclaim his glorious praise.

Say to God: How tremendous your deeds are!
On account of your great strength
Your enemies woo your favour.

Let the whole earth worship you,
Singing praises, singing praises to your name.
Come and listen,
All you who fear God,
While I tell you what great things
He has done for me.

To him I cried aloud,
High praise was on my tongue.

From his holy temple
He heard my voice,
My entreaty reached his ears.

Bless our God, you peoples,
Loudly proclaim his praise.

In him every race
In the world be blessed;
All nations shall proclaim his glory.

Blessed be the Lord, the God of Israel
Who alone does wondrous deeds.

St Francis of Assisi (1181–1226)

Signs of conversion

Jonathan Edwards, the eighteenth-century American preacher, sought to define the signs of authentic conversion. While he affirmed that, once saved, converts cannot lose their salvation, he recognised the problem posed by seeing apparent converts exhibit no evidence of changed lives. He wrote the book, Religious Affections, *in part to address this question and his central argument was that true religion largely consists of holy affections, which he defined as natural and intense reactions – either positive or negative – to things of real consequence to us. Edwards believed that these holy affections will be visible and obvious.*

Gracious affections have efficacy, because of the transcendent excellence of divine things. These are intrinsic in themselves, and bear no conceived relation to self or to self-interest. It is this that causes men to be holy in all their practice. In turn this helps them to persevere all the time. For the nature of religion is invariably always the same, at all times, and through all changes. It never alters in any respect. The foundation of all holy affections is in moral excellence and the beauty of holiness. There is a love of holiness for its own sake that inclines people to practice holiness. Holiness is thus the main business that excites, draws, and governs all gracious affections. No wonder then that all such affections tend to holiness, for men will be united to and possessed by that which they love and desire.

Jonathan Edwards (1703–1758)

Slow us down

Peter Marshall was born in Scotland but emigrated to America, where he was ordained. He was appointed chaplain to the Senate and was admired for the sincerity and simplicity of his daily opening prayers.

In the name of Jesus Christ, who was never in a hurry, we pray, O God, that Thou wilt slow us down, for we know that we live too fast. With all of eternity before us, make us take time to live – time to get acquainted with Thee, time to enjoy Thy blessings, and time to know each other.

Peter Marshall (1902–1949)

Smile at someone

Mother Teresa was born in Albania, received some of her education in Ireland and went to India at the age of nineteen. She took her religious vows two years later and dedicated the rest of her life to caring for the poor and needy in India. This brief quotation reminds us of the special affirmation it gives someone when we stop and smile at them.

Every time you smile at someone, it is an action of love, a gift to that person, a beautiful thing.

Mother Teresa (1910–1997)

Solomon's wisdom

The Epistle of Privy Counsel is believed to have been written by the same anonymous author as The Cloud of Unknowing. *It was addressed to a particular person, but its recipient was unnamed. Here the recipient is reminded of how Solomon achieved great wisdom – and that one of the first signs of being wise is to recognize that wisdom does not consist of intellect or knowledge.*

That wise man, Solomon, warmly recommends this simple and delightful exercise. Basically it is the supreme Wisdom of God coming down graciously into a man's soul, joining it in union to himself in simplicity and prudence ... he is a happy man who finds this unifying wisdom; who succeeds in his spiritual exercises through this loving simplicity and spiritual insight; who offers up to God the blind awareness of his own being; who puts far behind him all his scholarly knowledge and questionings, intellectual and natural alike. Getting hold of this spiritual wisdom by this simple exercise is better than getting gold or silver.

Anon. (14th century)

The soul

Albert Schweitzer was a theologian, musician, philosopher and doctor. He received the 1952 Nobel Peace Prize for his philosophy of 'reverence for life' most notably shown in his founding of a hospital in Gabon, West Africa.

What does the word 'soul' mean? ... No one can give a definition of the soul. But we know what it feels like. The soul is the sense of something higher than ourselves, something that stirs in us thoughts, hopes, and aspirations which go out to the world of goodness, truth, and beauty. The soul is a burning desire to breathe in this world of light and never to lose it – to remain children of light.

Albert Schweitzer (1875–1965)

Speak to us of prayer

Kahlil Gibran, a poet, artist and writer, was born in Lebanon but spent most of his life in America. His best-known work was The Prophet, *from which the following reflection on prayer is taken.*

Then a Priestess said, Speak to us of Prayer.

And he answered, saying:

You pray in your distress and in your need; would that you might pray also in the fullness of your joy and in your days of abundance.

For what is prayer but the expansion of yourself into the living ether?

And if it is your comfort to pour your darkness into space, it is for your delight to pour forth the dawning of your heart.

And if you cannot but weep when your soul summons you to prayer, she should spur you again and yet again, though weeping, until you shall come laughing.

When you pray you rise to meet in the air those who are praying at that very hour, and whom save in prayer you may not meet.

Therefore let your visit to that temple invisible be for naught but ecstasy and sweet communion.

For if you should enter the temple for no other purpose than asking you shall not receive:

And if you should enter into it to humble yourself you shall not be lifted:

Or even if you should enter into it to beg for the good of others you shall not be heard.

It is enough that you enter the temple invisible.

I cannot teach you how to pray in words.

God listens not to your words save when he himself utters them through your lips.

And I cannot teach you the prayer of the seas and the forests and the mountains.

But you who are born of the mountains and the forests and the seas can find their prayer in your heart,

And if you but listen in the stillness of the night you shall hear them saying in silence,

'Our God, who art our winged self, it is thy will in us that willeth.

'It is thy desire in us that desireth.

'It is thy urge in us that would turn our nights, which are thine, into days which are thine also.

'We cannot ask thee for aught, for thou knowest our needs before they are born in us:

'Thou art our need; and in giving us more of thyself thou givest us all.'

Kahlil Gibran (1883–1931)

Spiritual trials

François Fénelon was a French Roman Catholic theologian, poet and writer. He was ordained at about the age of twenty-four and joined a religious Order. He became an advocate of Quietism, which emphasized intellectual stillness and interior passivity as essential conditions of perfection.

God, who could have saved us without crosses, has not wished to do so ... In this he is the master. We have only to be silent, and to adore his profound wisdom without understanding it. What we see clearly is that we cannot become entirely good except as we become humble, disinterested, detached from ourselves, in order to relate everything to God without any turning back upon ourselves.

François Fénelon (1651–1715)

St Aidan's prayer

Aidan was an Irish monk at the monastery on the island of Iona in Scotland. When sent to Northumbria at the request of King Oswald he chose the island of Lindisfarne as his base and established a monastery there.

Lord, this bare island, make it a place of peace.
Here be the peace of those who do thy will.
Here be the peace of brother serving man.
Here be the peace of holy monks obeying.
Here be the peace of praise by dark and day.
Be this island thy holy island.
I, Lord, thy servant, Aidan, make this prayer.
Be it thy care.
Amen.

St Aidan (d. 651)

Stand up and be counted

Alan Paton was a South African teacher who objected to the apartheid legislation in that country. He wrote a number of novels, the best-known of which is Cry, the Beloved Country, *dealing with the racial situation in South Africa. This prayer expresses the cost of commitment both to God and our fellow human beings.*

Give us courage, O Lord, to stand up and be counted, to stand up for those who cannot stand up for themselves. To stand up for ourselves when it is needful to do so. Let us fear nothing more than we fear thee. Let us love nothing more than we love thee, for then we shall fear nothing also. Let us have no other god before thee, whether nation or party or state or church. Let us seek no other peace but the peace which is thine, and make us its instruments, opening our eyes and our ears and our hearts, so that we should know always what work of peace we should do for thee.

Alan Paton (1903–1988)

Steer by the Bible

Henry Ward Beecher was the brother of Harriet Beecher Stowe, the author of Uncle Tom's Cabin. *A prominent American Congregationalist clergyman and speaker in the mid- to late nineteenth century, he was pastor of a large church in Brooklyn.*

The Bible is God's chart for you to steer by, to keep you from the bottom of the sea, and to show you where the harbour is, and how to reach it without running on rocks and bars.

Henry Ward Beecher (1813–1887)

A stolen book

The Desert Fathers chose to live the life of hermits in the desert in order to reclaim a faith that had become institutionalized after the conversion of Constantine and the adoption of Christianity by the Roman Empire. Many of their writings date from the fourth century and Thomas Merton, a twentieth-century Catholic monk with a particular interest in mysticism, collected a number of them together in his book Sayings of the Desert Fathers.

Abbot Anastasius had a book written on very fine parchment which was worth eighteen pence, and had in it both the Old and New Testaments in full. Once a certain brother came to visit him, and seeing the book made off with it. So that day when Abbot Anastasius went to read his book, and found that it was gone, he realised that the brother had taken it. But he did not send after him to inquire about it for fear that the brother might add perjury to theft. Well, the brother went down into the nearby city in order to sell the book. And the price he asked was sixteen pence. The buyer said: Give me the book that I may find out whether it is worth that much. With that, the buyer took the book to the holy Anastasius and said: Father, take a look at this book, please, and tell me whether you think I ought to buy it for sixteen pence. Is it worth that much? Abbot Anastasius said: Yes, it is a fine book, it is worth that much. So the buyer went back to the brother and said: Here is your money. I showed the book to Abbot Anastasius and he said it is a fine book and is worth at least sixteen pence. But the brother asked: Was that all he said? Did he make any other remarks? No, said the buyer, he did not say another word. Well, said the brother, I have changed my mind and I don't want to sell this book after all. Then he hastened to Abbot Anastasius and begged him with tears to take back his book, but the Abbot would not accept it, saying, Go in peace, brother, I make you a present of it. But the brother said: If you do not take it back I shall never have any peace. After that the brother dwelt with Abbot Anastasius for the rest of his life.

Thomas Merton (1915–1968)

Strengthen me, O God

Thomas à Kempis was a Catholic monk and author of what is possibly the best-known book on Christian devotion, The Imitation of Christ. *This prayer seeks God's help for power to focus only on him.*

Strengthen me, O God, by the grace of your Holy Spirit; grant me to be strengthened with the might of the inner man, and to put away from my heart all useless anxiety and distress, and let me never be distracted by various longings, whether they are worthless or precious; but may I view all things as passing away, and myself as passing with them.

Grant me prudently to avoid the one who flatters me, and patiently to bear with the one who contradicts me; for it is a mark of great wisdom not to be moved by every wind of words or to be influenced by wicked flattery; for thus we will go on securely in the course we have begun.

Thomas à Kempis (c. 1380–1471)

Suffering leads to hope

The apostle Paul wrote to the Christian congregations in Rome during the first century of the church and part of his message is to encourage his readers who may face very difficult times ahead because of their faith.

And not only that, but we also boast in our sufferings, knowing that suffering produces endurance, and endurance produces character, and character produces hope, and hope does not disappoint us, because God's love has been poured into our hearts through the Holy Spirit that has been given to us.

Romans 5:3–5, NRSV

The suffering servant

In this song, Isaiah writes about the intense suffering of the coming servant. The pronouns he, him, we, our *and* us *are significant. His suffering has a deep meaning: he bore our pain, which was the punishment due to us for our sin and the price he paid for our salvation. Christians see this prophecy as fulfilled in the death of Jesus Christ on the cross.*

Who has believed what we have heard?
And to whom has the arm of the LORD been revealed?
For he grew up before him like a young plant,
and like a root out of dry ground;
he had no form or majesty that we should look at him,
nothing in his appearance that we should desire him.
He was despised and rejected by others;
a man of suffering and acquainted with infirmity;
and as one from whom others hide their faces
he was despised, and we held him of no account.

Surely he has borne our infirmities
and carried our diseases;
yet we accounted him stricken,
struck down by God, and afflicted.
But he was wounded for our transgressions,
crushed for our iniquities;
upon him was the punishment that made us whole,
and by his bruises we are healed.
All we like sheep have gone astray;
we have all turned to our own way,
and the LORD has laid on him
the iniquity of us all.

He was oppressed, and he was afflicted,
yet he did not open his mouth;
like a lamb that is led to the slaughter,
and like a sheep that before its shearers is silent,
so he did not open his mouth.
By a perversion of justice he was taken away.
Who could have imagined his future?
For he was cut off from the land of the living,
stricken for the transgression of my people.
They made his grave with the wicked
and his tomb with the rich,
although he had done no violence,
and there was no deceit in his mouth.

Yet it was the will of the LORD to crush him with pain.
When you make his life an offering for sin,
he shall see his offspring, and shall prolong his days;
through him the will of the LORD shall prosper.
Out of his anguish he shall see light;
he shall find satisfaction through his knowledge.
The righteous one, my servant, shall make many righteous,
and he shall bear their iniquities.
Therefore I will allot him a portion with the great,
and he shall divide the spoil with the strong;
because he poured out himself to death,
and was numbered with the transgressors;
yet he bore the sin of many,
and made intercession for the transgressors.

Isaiah 53, NRSV

Take warning

John Betjeman was a poet, writer and broadcaster. An unsuccessful student at Oxford, he was many years later awarded an honorary doctorate there. He was made Poet Laureate in 1972. A practising Anglican, his religious beliefs come through in some of his poems, albeit sometimes in a rather light-hearted way. The following extract is from the close of a long poem entitled 'Blame the Vicar'.

Dear readers, from this rhyme take warning,
And if you heard the bell this morning
Your vicar went to pray for you,
A task the Prayer Book bids him do.
'Highness' or 'Lowness' do not matter,
You are the Church and must not scatter,
Cling to the Sacraments and pray
And God be with you every day.

John Betjeman (1906–1984)

Teach us to pray

Eric Milner-White was Dean of King's College, Cambridge from just after the First World War until 1941. One of his lasting achievements while at the college was to introduce the Service of Nine Lessons and Carols, first broadcast in by the BBC in 1928 and still a feature of the BBC's Christmas schedule.

Lord, teach us to pray.
Help us to come with boldness to the throne of grace.
Make us conscious of your presence in our midst.
Give us the freedom of the Holy Spirit.
Enlarge our vision and increase our faith.
And may our words and thoughts be now acceptable in your
   sight.
O God, our rock and our redeemer.

Eric Milner-White (1884–1963)

The teaching of the apostles

The Didache is a collection of teachings to the early church. It was mentioned in a number of fourth-century writings but was thought to have been lost until a discovery, in the nineteenth century, of documents dating from the eleventh century in which the Didache was recorded.

My child, thou shalt remember him that speaketh unto thee the word of God night and day, and shalt honour him as the Lord; for whencesoever the Lordship speaketh, there is the Lord.

Moreover thou shalt seek out day by day the persons of the saints, that thou mayest find rest in their words.

Thou shalt not make a schism, but thou shalt pacify them that contend; thou shalt judge righteously, thou shalt not make a difference in a person to reprove him for transgressions.

Thou shalt not doubt whether a thing shall be or not be.

Be not thou found holding out thy hands to receive, but drawing them in as to giving.

If thou hast ought passing through thy hands, thou shalt give a ransom for thy sins.

Thou shalt not hesitate to give, neither shalt thou murmur when giving; for thou shalt know who is the good paymaster of thy reward.

Thou shalt not turn away from him that is in want, but shalt make thy brother partaker in all things, and shalt not say that anything is thy own. For if ye are fellow-partakers in that which is imperishable, how much rather in the things which are perishable?

Thou shalt not withhold thy hand from thy son or from thy daughter, but from their youth thou shalt teach them the fear of God.

Thou shalt not command thy bondservant or thine handmaid in thy bitterness who trust in the same God as thyself, lest haply they should cease to fear the God who is over both of you; for He cometh, not to call men with respect of persons, but He cometh to those whom the Spirit hath prepared.

But ye, servants, shall be subject unto your masters, as to a type of God, in shame and fear.

Thou shalt hate all hypocrisy, and everything that is not pleasing to the Lord.

Thou shalt never forsake the commandments of the Lord but shalt keep those things which thou hast received, neither adding to them nor taking away from them.

In church thou shalt confess thy transgressions, and shalt not betake thyself to prayer with an evil conscience. This is the way of life.

Didache (1st–2nd century)

The telephone

Michel Quoist is a French parish priest and theologian best known for his devotional work Prayers of Life. *This prayer is a reflection on the importance of real listening in effective communication.*

I have just hung up; why did he telephone?
I don't know ...
O! I get it ... I talked a lot and listened little.
Forgive me, Lord, it was a monologue and not a dialogue.
I explained my idea and did not get his;
Since I didn't listen, I learned nothing,
Since I didn't listen, I didn't help,
Since I didn't listen, we didn't communicate.
Forgive me, Lord, for we were connected, and now we are
cut off.

Michel Quoist (b. 1921)

Thank God

Michael Counsell is an Anglican clergyman who trained as a scientist before he was ordained and has worked overseas for much of his life. He has written a number of books. This is a modern prayer of confession and thanksgiving.

Lord, you call us to confess our sins,
But I don't often tell you what a fool I've been.
It would be a relief to tell someone.
So many things I could have done for you,
But I failed, by making senseless decisions.
I tried to speak your word, but it was misunderstood,
Because I expressed it foolishly.
I have harmed other people, when I was too stupid
to foresee the effects of what I had done;
and broken fellowship with them, through not knowing
how silly my speech would sound.
Lord, how can you love such a fool?
And yet, foolish as it may seem, I really believe you do love
    me.
Do you? You do! Thank God. Amen.

Michael Counsell (b. 1935)

Thanking God

*German pastor Dietrich Bonhoeffer was a leader in the Confessing Church,
which opposed the anti-Semitic policies of Adolf Hitler during the Second
World War. He was hanged just weeks before the liberation of Berlin by the
Allies. This extract reminds us of the need to express our gratitude to God for
the small things of life that we receive from him.*

Only he who gives thanks for little things receives big things.
We prevent God from giving us the great spiritual gifts he has in
store for us, because we do not give thanks for daily gifts. We
think we dare not be satisfied with the small measure of spiritual
knowledge, experience, and love that has been given to us, and
that we must constantly be looking forward eagerly for the
highest good. Then we deplore the fact that we lack the deep
certainty, the strong faith, and the rich experience that God has
given to others, and we consider this lament to be pious. We
pray for the big things and forget to give thanks for the ordinary,
small (and yet not so small) gifts. How can God entrust great
things to one who will not thankfully receive from him the little
things?

Dietrich Bonhoeffer (1906–1945)

Thanksgiving

Following the restoration of the monarchy the new prayer book of 1662 was produced. However, clerics in the Church of England proposed that revisions should be made to the Book of Common Prayer *to make it acceptable to Protestant non-conformists. The proposed prayer book never received wide publication because, when William and Mary came to the throne, the non-conformists no longer wanted to be have any part in the Church of England but sought to be tolerated as separate instead. This thanksgiving comes from the 1689 revision.*

Almighty God, Father of all mercies, we your unworthy servants give you most humble and hearty thanks for all your goodness and loving-kindness to us and to all people; we bless you for our creation, preservation, and all the blessings of this life; but above all for your inestimable love in the redemption of the world by our Lord Jesus Christ, for the means of grace, and for the hope of glory. And we beseech you, give us that due sense of all your mercies, that our hearts may be unfeignedly thankful, and that we show forth your praise, not only with our lips, but in our lives; by giving up ourselves to your service, and by walking before you in holiness and righteousness all our days; through Jesus Christ our Lord, to whom with you and the Holy Ghost be all honour and glory, world without end. Amen.

Proposed Book of Common Prayer (1689)

Thirst relieved

John Charles Ryle was a minister for almost forty years before becoming the first Bishop of Liverpool in 1880, at the recommendation of the Prime Minister, Benjamin Disraeli.

'In the last day, that great day of the feast, Jesus stood and cried, saying, "If any man thirst, let him come unto Me, and drink. He that believeth on Me, as the Scripture hath said, out of his belly shall flow rivers of living water"' (John 7:37, 38) ... In this evil world you may not perhaps feel all the sensible comfort you could desire. But remember you cannot have two heavens. Perfect happiness is yet to come. The devil is not yet bound. There is a good time coming for all who feel their sins and come to Christ, and commit their thirsting souls to his keeping. When he comes again they will be completely satisfied. They will remember all the way by which they were led, and see the need-be of everything that befell them. Above all, they will wonder that they could ever live so long without Christ, and hesitate about coming to him.

There is a pass in Scotland called Glencroe, which supplies a beautiful illustration of what heaven will be to the souls who come to Christ. The road through Glencroe carries the traveller up a long and steep ascent, with many a little turn and winding in its course. But when the top of the pass is reached, a stone is seen by the wayside with these simple words inscribed upon it: 'Rest and be thankful.' Those words describe the feelings with which every thirsting one who comes to Christ will enter heaven.

J C Ryle (1816–1900)

258 ✣ BEST LOVED PRAYERS AND WORDS OF WISDOM

Three ways to look

Regarded by many as the Billy Graham of the nineteenth century, Dwight Moody was an American evangelist and publisher. He became well known in England as a result of a preaching trip in 1872, which he undertook together with the Gospel singer Ira Sankey. Together they produced books of hymns. The passage here comes from one of Moody's books, The Way to God.

Someone has said: 'There are three ways to look. If you want to be wretched, look within; if you wish to be distracted, look around; but if you would have peace, look up.'

'Peter looked away from Christ, and he immediately began to sink. The Master said to him: O thou of little faith! Wherefore didst thou doubt?' (Matthew 14:31).

He had God's eternal word, which was sure footing, and better than either marble, granite, or iron; but the moment he took his eyes off Christ, down he went. Those who look around cannot see how unstable and dishonouring is their walk. We want to look straight at the 'Author and Finisher of our faith' (Hebrews 12:2).

When I was a boy I could only make a straight track in the snow, by keeping my eyes fixed upon a tree or some object before me. The moment I took my eye off the mark set in front of me, I walked crooked. It is only when we look fixedly on Christ that we find perfect peace. After he rose from the dead he showed his disciples his hands and his feet.

'Behold my hands and my feet, that it is I myself: handle me, and see; for a spirit hath not flesh and bones, as ye see me have' (Luke 24:39).

That was the ground of their peace. If you want to scatter your doubts, look at the blood; and if you want to increase your doubts, look at yourself. You will get doubts enough for years by being occupied with yourself for a few days.

Then again: look at what he is, and at what he has done; not at what you are, and what you have done. That is the way to get peace and rest.

Dwight L Moody (1837–1899)

Time as gift

In Receiving the Day, *a book that identifies specific practices for ordering the day, the week, the year, and the lifetime – practices that enable us to live more richly and rightly in time – Dorothy Bass seeks to restore a sense of wonder in our relationship with the larger order in the universe.*

To know time as gift is to know that its basic rhythms and inevitable passing are beyond our control. And to know time as a gift is to recognise time as the setting within which we also receive God's other gifts, including the fruits of nature and the companionship of one another. To help one another to this knowledge is blessing indeed.

Dorothy C Bass (b. 1949)

A time for everything

In the book of Ecclesiastes, part of the wisdom literature of the Old Testament, the writer reflects on the varying seasons of human existence and the fact that there are certain occasions where a particular action is appropriate.

For everything there is a season, and a time for every matter under heaven:
a time to be born, and a time to die;
a time to plant, and a time to pluck up what is planted;
a time to kill, and a time to heal;
a time to break down, and a time to build up;
a time to weep, and a time to laugh;
a time to mourn, and a time to dance;
a time to throw away stones, and a time to gather stones together;
a time to embrace, and a time to refrain from embracing;
a time to seek, and a time to lose;
a time to keep, and a time to throw away;
a time to tear, and a time to sew;
a time to keep silence, and a time to speak;
a time to love, and a time to hate;
a time for war, and a time for peace.

Ecclesiastes 3:1–8, NRSV

Time is precious

The Cloud of Unknowing is a practical spiritual guidebook thought to have been written in the latter half of the fourteenth century by an anonymous English monk, possibly a Carthusian, who counsels a young student to seek God not through knowledge but through love.

Be attentive to time and how you spend it. Nothing is more precious. This is evident when you recall that in one tiny moment heaven may be gained or lost. God, the master of time, never gives the future. He gives only the present, moment by moment.

Anon. (14th century)

Traditional Gaelic prayer

This prayer, recorded by the Northumbria Community, was learned from a fish salter on the island of Barra.

As it was, as it is,
And as it shall be evermore,
God of grace, God in Trinity!
With the ebb, with the flow, ever it is so,
God of grace, O Trinity,
With the ebb and flow.

Anon.

Trinity Sunday

George Herbert, remembered as a writer of religious poems, was a member of parliament and later an ordained priest. This poem, 'Trinity Sunday', is from his work The Temple.

Lord, who hast formed me out of mud,
And hast redeemed me through thy blood
And sanctified me to do good;

Purge all my sins done heretofore;
For I confess my heavy score,
And I will strive to sin no more.

Enrich my heart, mouth, hands in me,
With faith, with hope, with charity;
That I may run, rise, rest with thee.

George Herbert (1593–1633)

Trust in the favour of God

William Tyndale was a gifted linguist and he believed that everyone should have access to the Scriptures in their native language. His translation of the New Testament into English appeared in 1525–26 and he translated much of the Old Testament from the original Hebrew. English Bibles were prohibited at the time and eventually Tyndale was arrested and imprisoned in horrible conditions. He was tried for heresy and treason in an unfair trial, and convicted. Tyndale was then strangled and burnt at the stake in a Brussels prison yard on 6 October 1536.

Faith is, then, a lively and steadfast trust in the favour of God, wherewith we commit ourselves altogether unto God. And that trust is so surely grounded and sticks so fast in our hearts, that a man would not once doubt of it, although he should die a thousand times therefor. And such trust, wrought by the Holy Ghost through faith, makes a man glad, lusty, cheerful and true-hearted unto God and unto all creatures.

William Tyndale (1494–1536)

Tyndale's last words

William Tyndale was martyred for his faith in 1536. His last words were a prayer that was answered three years later, in the publication of King Henry VIII's 1539 English 'Great Bible'.

Lord, open the king of England's eyes.
William Tyndale (1494–1536)

Understanding the gospel

Lesslie Newbigin was a Presbyterian minister who worked in India as a missionary for many years. However, he is best remembered for the period following his retirement when he tried to communicate the need for the church to take the gospel again to a post-Christian Western culture. Some of his most important work was written during this time.

The truth is that we do not truly understand the gospel if we spend all our time preaching it to Christians ... The gospel is communication of news to those who do not know it, and we only really understand it as we are involved in so communicating it.

Lesslie Newbigin (1909–1998)

Unity

The letter to the Ephesian church was written to encourage the Christians there. As tensions and divisions were threatening the church, they are reminded of all that should keep them in fellowship with each other, and all that should keep them united.

... lead a life worthy of the calling to which you have been called, with all humility and gentleness, with patience, bearing with one another in love, making every effort to maintain the unity of the Spirit in the bond of peace. There is one body and one Spirit, just as you were called to the one hope of your calling, one Lord, one faith, one baptism, one God and Father of all, who is above all and through all and in all.

Ephesians 4:1–6, NRSV

Unity at the breaking of bread

The Didache is a collection of teachings to the early church. It was mentioned in a number of fourth-century writings. It includes this prayer for Christian unity at the breaking of bread.

As the grain from which the bread we break was made
Were once scattered over the fields,
And then gathered together and made one,
So may your Church be gathered from all over the earth
Into your kingdom.

Didache (1st–2nd century)

Unknowable God

In his letter to the Romans, the apostle Paul affirms that God in his mercy offers salvation to all. This prompts this exuberant outpouring of praise.

O the depth of the riches and wisdom and knowledge of God! How unsearchable are his judgements and how inscrutable his ways!

'For who has known the mind of the Lord? Or who has been his counsellor?'

'Or who has given a gift to him, to receive a gift in return?' For from him and through him and to him are all things. To him be the glory for ever. Amen.

Romans 11:33–36, NRSV

Vain repentance

Like his younger brother John Wesley, Charles was a leader of the Methodist movement. He is remembered chiefly for the many hymns he wrote, a number of which are still regularly sung today. All Christians must surely identify with his words, as he confesses that committing the same sins over and again robs him of spiritual peace, which he longs to know again.

Times without number have I prayed,
'This only once forgive';
Relapsing, when thy hand was stayed,
And suffered me to live: –

Yet now the kingdom of thy peace,
Lord, to my heart restore;
Forgive my vain repentances,
And bid me sin no more.

Charles Wesley (1707–1788)

Warm your hearts

Thomas Watson was an English Puritan non-conformist preacher and author. Despite his Puritan views he supported the king and was briefly imprisoned under Cromwell. He went on to achieve fame and popularity as a preacher until the Restoration, following which he had to exercise his ministry privately until the 1672 Declaration of Indulgence which allowed him to obtain a licence to preach publicly again. This extract from his writing recalls the words of Cleopas and his companion after meeting the resurrected Jesus on the road to Emmaus (Luke 24:32).

Meditate for as long as it takes for you to find your heart warm. Don't leave off reading the Bible till you find your hearts warmed. Let the Bible not only inform you, but let it also inflame you ... Christian, if your heart is cold, stand at the fire of meditation until you find your affections warmed, and you are made fit for spiritual service.

Thomas Watson (c. 1620–1686)

The way, the truth and the life

Erasmus was a leading scholar of his day. He was critical of a number of the Christian practices and beliefs current at that time but unlike many other Reformers he did not join the Protestants, but remained committed to the Catholic Church. He nevertheless had considerable sympathy with many of Martin Luther's criticisms of the Church.

Lord Jesus Christ,
You have said that you are the Way,
The Truth and the Life.
Suffer us not to stray from you, who are the Way,
Nor to distrust you, who are the Truth,
Nor to rest in anything other than you,
Who are the Life.
Amen.

Desiderius Erasmus (1466–1536)

We cannot avoid temptation

Thomas à Kempis was a Catholic monk and author of what is possibly the best-known book on Christian devotion, The Imitation of Christ. *In this passage the author addresses the struggle that everyone faces with temptation.*

No one is completely free of temptations because the source of temptation is in ourselves. We were born in sinful desire. When one temptation passes, another is on its way. We will always have temptation because we are sinners who lost our original innocence in the Garden. Many have tried to escape temptations only to find that they more grievously fall into them. We cannot win this battle by running away alone; the key to victory is true humility and patience; in them we overcome the enemy.

If we merely turn away from temptation outwardly and do not strike at the root, we will make very little progress. In fact, you will find that the temptations will return even more quickly and powerfully, and you will feel even worse. Little by little, through patient endurance of spirit (with the help of god), you will win a better victory than by your own determination.

Thomas à Kempis (c. 1380–1471)

What do I love?

Born in present-day Algeria, Augustine was educated in North Africa and went on to become a bishop in the church there. He is most famous for his autobiographical Confessions. *This quotation is a meditation on what it means to love God. Such love is strong and lasting; it is distinctive and spiritual.*

And what do I love when I love you? Not physical beauty, or the grandeur of our existence in time, or the radiance of light that pleases the eye, or the sweet melody of old familiar songs, or the fragrance of flowers and ointments and spices, or the taste of manna or honey, or the arms we use to clasp each other. None of these do I love when I love my God. Yet, there is a kind of light, and a kind of melody, and a kind of fragrance, and a kind of food, and a kind of embracing when I love my God. They are the kind of light and sound and odour and food and love that affect the senses of the inner man. There is another dimension of life in which my soul reflects a light that space itself cannot contain. It hears melodies that never fade with time. It inhales lovely scents that are not blown away by the wind. It eats without diminishing or consuming the supply. It never gets separated from the embrace of God and never gets tired of it. That is what I love when I love my God.

St Augustine of Hippo (354–430)

What is prayer?

*Charles Browne was a twentieth-century priest and writer. He was
particularly interested in the nature of religious language.*

What am I doing when I am praying? It is well not to be too
curious. No man can think and pray at the same time and do
both well.

What we do when we are not praying shapes what we do
when we pray. What we do when we are praying shapes what we
do when we are not praying. Theology safeguards these facts
with its emphasis on man's responsibility for his actions.

Individuals, the world and the church live and move and
have their being in God.

I do not believe in God because I believe in the world; I
believe in the world because I believe in God who loves the
world. I do not believe in God because I believe in the church; I
believe in the church because I believe in God. ... When I pray
for the church and the world I find that I am praying for myself,
and when I pray for myself I find that I am praying for the world
and the church.

'Those whom God hath joined together let no man put
asunder.' The individual, the world and the church are one in
God.

In God all things have their origin; he is to be thought of as
the maker of words, bread, wine and prayers – all our operations
are co-operations with him, and though the help we give him is
fragmentary we know that fragmentary help is real help.

... Jesus said: 'When you pray, go into your room and shut
the door and pray to your Father who is in secret; and your
Father who is in secret will reward you.'

God became man without ceasing to be God that men might
be godly without ceasing to be men.

R E Charles Browne (1906–1975)

What is religion?

A number of writers, from Latin poets to nineteenth-century satirists and philosophers, have attempted to define religion or its effects, but the defining statement comes from the Letter of James.

Religion that is pure and undefiled before God, the Father, is this: to care for orphans and widows in their distress, and to keep oneself unstained by the world.

James 1:27, NRSV

What makes you come alive?

Howard Thurman was an American writer, philosopher, civil-rights leader and theologian. He was ordained as a Baptist minister in 1925 and went on to write many books. He was a classmate and friend of Martin Luther King Sr, and mentored Martin Luther King Jr when he was at Boston University.

Don't ask yourself what the world needs. Ask yourself what makes you come alive and then go do that. Because what the world needs is people who have come alive.

Howard Thurman (1899–1981)

What we will be

The writer of 1 John, probably not the apostle John, writes to an unspecified group of Christians, mainly on the themes of certainty and assurance. We cannot yet know the future but we should live in the knowledge that we have been adopted into God's family.

Beloved, we are God's children now; what we will be has not yet been revealed. What we do know is this: when he is revealed, we will be like him, for we will see him as he is.

1 John 3:2, NRSV

When Jesus came to Birmingham

In his poem 'Indifference', Geoffrey Studdert Kennedy compares the behaviour of Jesus' contemporaries with ours towards the stranger and the outcast. In Matthew's Gospel (25:31–46), Jesus tells his followers that they will be judged according to how they have treated those who are in need.

When Jesus came to Golgotha they hanged him on a tree,
They drave great nails through hands and feet, and made a
    Calvary;
They crowned him with a crown of thorns, red were his
    wounds and deep,
For those were crude and cruel days, and human flesh was
    cheap.

When Jesus came to Birmingham they simply passed him by,
They never hurt a hair of him, they only let him die;
For men had grown more tender, and they would not give
    him pain,
They only just passed down the street, and left him in the
    rain.

Still Jesus cried, 'Forgive them, for they know not what they
    do,'
And still it rained the wintry rain that drenched him through
    and through;
The crowds went home and left the streets without a soul to
    see,
And Jesus crouched against a wall and cried for Calvary.

G A Studdert Kennedy (1883–1929)

When you feel depressed

Martin Manser is a reference-book editor and language trainer. He has compiled or edited many reference books including titles that encourage Bible reading. He has also written a book of prayers from the heart, from which this extract is quoted.

I feel isolated, Lord. You seem a million miles away. At times I can't stop myself from crying; I feel so overwhelmed, worn out and torn apart within me. Everything has got on top of me. To be honest, I don't know who to turn to. I don't feel really close to anyone I can open up to and say what's really going on inside me.

Lord, I know the theory! You're supposed to be my rock, but all the bottled-up feelings are still there.

There were of course the good old days when my faith – and perhaps it was that rather than you – kept me going, smiling happily and not letting anything bother me.

Lord, if you could help me to be a little less preoccupied with myself I'd be so thankful. May I learn to think, to realize that feelings aren't facts, to be realistic, that I can't change the world overnight. Lord, help me to be patient with those around me ... my circumstances ... and also myself. Help me to be firm, too, Lord, if possible, to move on and to move out from the endless despair I feel I'm stuck in right now.

May I remember again you sympathize with and understand what I am going through – that Lord Jesus, you felt abandoned on the cross.

Please restore in me the right perspective on life. Help me to control my anxieties. Give me people I can really talk to.

Please come and help me, Lord. Give me strength for one day at a time.

Martin Manser (b. 1952)

Who will separate us from the love of Christ?

If God is with you then nothing can prevail against you. In Romans chapter 8 the apostle Paul reassures his readers that, whatever hardships or persecution the followers of Christ may face, the love of God is still with them.

What then are we to say about these things? If God is for us, who is against us? He who did not withhold his own Son, but gave him up for all of us, will he not with him also give us everything else? Who will bring any charge against God's elect? It is God who justifies. Who is to condemn? It is Christ Jesus, who died, yes, who was raised, who is at the right hand of God, who indeed intercedes for us. Who will separate us from the love of Christ? Will hardship, or distress, or persecution, or famine, or nakedness, or peril, or sword? As it is written,

'For your sake we are being killed all day long;
    we are accounted as sheep to be slaughtered.'
No, in all these things we are more than conquerors through him who loved us. For I am convinced that neither death, nor life, nor angels, nor rulers, nor things present, nor things to come, nor powers, nor height, nor depth, nor anything else in all creation, will be able to separate us from the love of God in Christ Jesus our Lord.

Romans 8:31–39, NRSV

Who would true valour see

These lines come from the end of Part 2 of The Pilgrim's Progress *(1684), by John Bunyan. They were adapted for inclusion in the 1906* English Hymnal.

Who would true valour see,
Let him come hither;
One here will constant be,
Come wind, come weather.
There's no discouragement
Shall make him once relent
His first avowed intent,
To be a pilgrim.

Whoso beset him round
With dismal stories,
Do but themselves confound,
His strength the more is.
No lion can him fright,
He'll with a giant fight,
But he will have a right
To be a pilgrim.

Hobgoblin, nor foul fiend,
Can daunt his spirit;
He knows, he at the end
Shall life inherit.
Then fancies fly away,
He'll fear not what men say,
He'll labour night and day
To be a pilgrim.

John Bunyan (1628–1688)

Wise men

It has been said that more books have been written about Martin Luther than about anyone else in history except for Jesus Christ. His ideas were central to the Protestant Reformation but here he points to the importance of the simple and the humble.

If we Christians would join the Wise Men, we must close our eyes to all that glitters before the world and look rather on the despised and foolish things, help the poor, comfort the despised, and aid the neighbour in his need.

Martin Luther (1483–1546)

The Word of God

John Stott is an Anglican clergyman noted as a key influence in the worldwide evangelical movement. He was ordained in 1945 and went on to become curate and then rector at All Souls, Langham Place, the church in which he had grown up, and in which he has spent almost all of his life.

We need to repent of the haughty way in which we sometimes stand in judgement upon Scripture and must learn to sit humbly under its judgement instead. If we come to Scripture with our minds made up, expecting to hear from it only an echo of our own thoughts and never the thunderclap of God's, then indeed he will not speak to us and we shall only be confirmed in our own prejudices. We must allow the Word of God to confront us, to disturb our security, to undermine our complacency and to overthrow our patterns of thought and behaviour.

John Stott (b. 1921)

The work of Christmas

Howard Thurman was ordained as a Baptist minister in 1925. He was an American writer, philosopher, civil-rights leader and theologian who wrote many books. He was a classmate and friend of Martin Luther King Sr, and mentored Martin Luther King Jr when he was at Boston University.

When the song of the angels is stilled,
When the star in the sky is gone,
When the kings and princes are home,
When the shepherds are back with their flock,
The work of Christmas begins:
To find the lost,
To heal the broken,
To feed the hungry,
To release the prisoner,
To rebuild the nations,
To bring peace among others,
To make music in the heart.

Howard Thurman (1899–1981)

The work of the Spirit

John Owen was a leading theologian in the time of Oliver Cromwell, whose 'New Model Army' was made up of men who held Puritan principles. Under Cromwell Owen was appointed dean of Christ Church, Oxford in 1651 and in 1652 he was made vice-chancellor.

I have only, then, to add the heads of the work of the Spirit in this business of mortification, which is so peculiarly ascribed to him.

In one word: This whole work, which I have described as our duty, is effected, carried on, and accomplished by the power of the Spirit ...

He alone clearly and fully convinces the heart of the evil and guilt and danger of the corruption, lust, or sin to be mortified ...

The Spirit alone reveals unto us the fullness of Christ for our relief ...

The Spirit alone establishes the heart in expectation of relief from Christ ...

The Spirit alone brings the cross of Christ into our hearts with its sin-killing power ...

The Spirit is the author and finisher of our sanctification.

John Owen (1616–1683)

The world in the heart

Thomas Watson was a seventeenth-century preacher, who was famous as the popular vicar of St Stephen's, Walbrook. He wrote a great deal, in a homely and clear style. His best known work is A Body of Divinity.

All the danger is when the world gets into the heart. The water is useful for the sailing of the ship; all the danger is when the water gets into the ship; so the fear is when the world gets into the heart. 'Thou shalt not covet.'

Thomas Watson (c. 1620–1686)

Worldly foolishness

John Trapp was an English Anglican Bible commentator. His large five-volume commentary is still read today and is known for its pithy statements and quotable prose. His volumes are quoted frequently by other religious writers, notably Charles Spurgeon.

They are fools that fear to lose their wealth by giving, but fear not to lose themselves by keeping it.

John Trapp (1601–1669)

Worshipping God

In the service of Holy Communion the congregation are called to praise God before confessing their sins and, in repentance, coming to the Lord's table to receive bread and wine.

Therefore with Angels and Archangels, and with all the company of heaven, we laud and magnify thy glorious Name; evermore praising thee, and saying, Holy, Holy, Holy, Lord God of, hosts, Heaven and earth are full of thy glory: Glory be to thee, O Lord Most High. Amen.

The Book of Common Prayer (1928)

You are holy

Francis of Assisi was a Roman Catholic friar and founder of the Franciscan Order. This prayer describes simply what God is like: his character and how we can know him personally.

You are holy, Lord, the only God,
And your deeds are wonderful.
You are strong.
You are great.
You are the most high.
You are almighty.
You, holy Father are King of heaven and earth.
You are three and one, Lord God, all Good.
You are Good, all Good, supreme Good.
Lord God, living and true.
You are love. You are wisdom.
You are humility. You are endurance.
You are rest. You are peace.
You are joy and gladness.
You are justice and moderation.
You are all our riches, and you suffice for us.
You are beauty.
You are gentleness.
You are our protector.
You are our guardian and defender.
You are our courage. You are our haven and our hope.
You are our faith, our great consolation.
You are our eternal life, great and wonderful Lord,
God almighty, merciful Saviour.

St Francis of Assisi (1181–1226)

Acknowledgements

Every effort has been made to trace copyright owners, and apologies are extended to anyone whose rights have inadvertently not been acknowledged. Omissions or inaccuracies of copyright will be corrected in any subsequent printings.

Apologist's evening prayer, The
Poems by C S Lewis copyright © C S Lewis Pte. Ltd. 1964.
Extracts reprinted by permission.

At the beginning of the day
Extracts from the *Book of Common Prayer*, the rights in which are vested in the Crown, are reproduced by permission of the Crown's Patentee, Cambridge University Press.

Be prepared for trials
The Quotable Saint (Checkmark Books, 2002).

Caring friendship
Excerpted from *Out of Solitude: Three Meditations on the Christian Life* by Henri J. M. Nouwen. Copyright ©1974, 2004 by Ave Maria Press, P.O. Box 428, Notre Dame, IN 46556, www.avemariapress.com. Used with permission of the publisher.

Christ's ladder to heaven
Henson, Herbert Hensley (1863–1947) in *Love's Redeeming Work* (OUP, 2001). Used with permission.

Circumstances
Excerpted from *The Life of Elijah* (Banner of Truth, 1963) available from www.banneroftruth.org.

Courage
Poems by C S Lewis copyright © C S Lewis Pte. Ltd. 1964.
Extracts reprinted by permission.

Acknowledgements

Discipleship
Taken from *My Utmost for His Highest* by Oswald Chambers, ©
1935 by Dodd Mead & Co., renewed © 1963 by the Oswald
Chambers Publications Assn., Ltd. Used by permission of
Discovery House Publishers, Grand Rapids MI 49501. All rights
reserved.

Dying well
The Quotable Saint (Checkmark Books, 2002).

Easter
Reproduced by kind permission of Continuum International
Publishing Group.

Easter Day
From Martin Manser, *Prayers for Good Times and Grim* (Monarch,
2008) with kind permission of Monarch.

Food for all
Copyright, Christian Aid. Used with permission. For more
information please visit www.christianaid.org.uk.

Forgetting myself
The extracts from the poem 'To Love – The Prayer of the
Adolescent' from Michel Quoist's *Prayers of Life* is reproduced
with the permission of the publishers Gill & Macmillan, Dublin.

Friendship
Moltmann, Jurgen (b. 1926) in *The Open Church* (SCM Press,
1978).

Gathered church, The
Paul, the Spirit, and the People of God copyright © 1993 by
Hendrickson Publishers, Inc., Peabody, Massachusetts. Used by
permission. All rights reserved.

Acknowledgements

Gloria in Excelsis
The Gloria as it appears in *Common Worship: Services and Prayers for the Church of England* (Church House Publishing, 2000) is copyright © The English Language Liturgical Consultation and is reproduced by permission of the publisher.

Go with the Lord
From *The Hodder Book of Prayers in Large Print* (Hodder & Stoughton, 1997). Printed with permission.

God cannot fail
Smith, Hannah Whitall (1832–1911), *All the Saints Adore Thee* (Baker, 1988).

God knows me
From *Knowing God*, J I Packer (Hodder & Stoughton, 1973). Printed with permission.

God of truth, deliver us
Permission sought from author's estate, but address not traced.

Good exchange, A
Elliot, Jim (1927–1956) *Journals of Jim Elliot* (Fleming H. Revell Company, 1983).

Grace, The
Extracts from the *Book of Common Prayer*, the rights in which are vested in the Crown, are reproduced by permission of the Crown's Patentee, Cambridge University Press.

Hope of the hopeless
Reproduced by kind permission of Continuum International Publishing Group.

I believe
Extracts from the *Book of Common Prayer*, the rights in which are vested in the Crown, are reproduced by permission of the Crown's Patentee, Cambridge University Press.

Acknowledgements

I want to love
The extracts from the poem 'To Love – The Prayer of the Adolescent' from Michel Quoist's *Prayers of Life* is reproduced with the permission of the publishers Gill & Macmillan, Dublin.

Importance of Christianity, The
God in the Dock by C S Lewis copyright © C S Lewis Pte. Ltd. 1970. Extracts reprinted by permission.

Into the desert
Reproduced by kind permission of Continuum International Publishing Group.

Jesus' hands
'Jesus' hands were kind hands' by Margaret Cropper (1886–1980). Reproduced by permission of Stainer & Bell Ltd, 23 Gruneisen Road, London, N3 1DZ, England.

Listening to that other voice
Mere Christianity by C S Lewis copyright © C S Lewis Pte. Ltd. 1942, 1943, 1944, 1952. Extracts reprinted by permission.

Lord's Prayer, The
Extracts from the *Book of Common Prayer*, the rights in which are vested in the Crown, are reproduced by permission of the Crown's Patentee, Cambridge University Press.

Love begins at home
From *Heart of Joy* (1987) edited by José Luis González-Baldo, reprinted with permission of St Anthony Messenger Press, 28 W.Liberty Street, Cincinnati, OH 45202.

Love is as hard as nails
Poems by C S Lewis copyright © C S Lewis Pte. Ltd. 1964. Extracts reprinted by permission.

Acknowledgements

Love's self-opening
Taylor, John Vernon (1914–2001) in *Love's Redeeming Work*
(OUP, 2001). Used with permission.

Loving God above all things
The prayer from *Common Worship: Services and Prayers for the Church of England* (Church House Publishing, 2000) is copyright © The Archbishop's Council 2000 and is reproduced by permission.

No mere religion
Stringfellow, William (1928–1985) in *Love's Redeeming Work* (OUP 2001). Used with permission.

Not to criticise
Taken from *My Utmost for His Highest* by Oswald Chambers, © 1935 by Dodd Mead & Co., renewed © 1963 by the Oswald Chambers Publications Assn., Ltd. Used by permission of Discovery House Publishers, Grand Rapids MI 49501. All rights reserved.

Opening the door to Christ
Stott, John (b. 1921) quoted in Timothy Dudley-Smith, *The Making of a Leader* (IVP, 1999).

Peace of mind
From *Strange Freedom: The Best of Howard Thurman on Religious Experience and Public Life* by Earl Fluker and Catherine Tumber Copyright © 1998 by Walter Earl Fluker and Catherine Tumber. Reprinted by permission of Beacon Press, Boston.

Prayer for humility
Barclay, William (1907–1978) in *SPCK Book of Christian Prayer* (SCM), used with permission from publisher.

Prayer for peace
Permission sought from Winston Press, the licensors, but address not traced.

Acknowledgements

Resurrection of Christ, The
Smith, Wilbur M (1894–1977) in *Therefore Stand: Christian Apologetics* (Baker Book House, 1965).

Serving
From *2000 Years of Prayer* (Canterbury Press, 1999) by permission of SPCK.

Slow us down
Permission sought from Catherine Marshall, the copyright holder, but address not traced.

Soul, The
Excerpt from *Reverence for life* (SPCK, 1970) with permission.

Stand up and be counted
Permission sought from Winston Press, the licensors, but address not traced.

Stolen book, A
Reproduced by kind permission of Continuum International Publishing Group.

Take warning
Reproduced by kind permission of Continuum International Publishing Group.

Teach us to pray
Eric Milner-White, *My God, My Glory* (SPCK), by permission of SPCK.

Thank God
Counsell, Michael, *2000 Years of Prayer* (Canterbury Press, 1999).

Thanking God
Bonhoeffer, Dietrich (1906–1945) *Life Together* (SCM, 1954).

Acknowledgements

Time as gift
Bass, Dorothy in *Receiving the Day*. Used with permission.

Understanding the gospel
Permission sought from Faith Press, the licensors, but address
not traced.

What is prayer?
Browne, R E Charles (1906–1975) in *Love's Redeeming Work*
(OUP, 2001). Used with permission.

When you feel depressed
From Martin Manser, *Prayers for Good Times and Grim* (Monarch,
2008) with kind permission of Monarch.

Word of God, The
Stott, John (b. 1921), *Authentic Christianity* (IVP, 1995).

Worshipping God
Extracts from the *Book of Common Prayer*, the rights in which are
vested in the Crown, are reproduced by permission of the
Crown's Patentee, Cambridge University Press.